ALL

IN

ALL IN:

Beat the Odds in Sales

By

B.O.L.O. Lee

ISBN-13:978-1983588464

For information, please contact BOLO Lee at BOLO@TheBoloGroup.com

www.thebologroup.com

The Contents

Acknowledgements

First, this book is dedicated to my little cousin, Keng Yang. You are loved and you are missed. Without you, this book and this direction in my life would not have happened. You will always live forever.

Second, thank you, Jerry Maras, may you rest in peace. You were a friend, brother, customer, mentor, and teacher. You taught me all about paint and how to play golf, but not just that, you taught me about life and focus. Always about focus - on the golf course and what's most important. You went out the only way you know how...birdie, birdie, eagle.

Most importantly, I would like to thank my wife, Ling, for her love, patience, support, strength, and undying belief in me. Without you supporting me through this journey, all of this would not be possible. It is true what they say, behind a strong man is an even stronger woman.

To my beautiful parents, Cha Vue and Cha Mee, no amount of appreciation and gratitude will ever be enough for what you have done for me and our family. From you, I've learned hard work, sacrifice, unconditional love, and the meaning of family. I will never be able to show you how much I appreciate the two of you and how proud I am to be able to have this one chance on this one planet to be born as your son, and to spend what little time we have together.

My Little Brother, Cha, thanks for loving me through thick and thin. I don't know how I deserve to have the best brother on earth, but I am proud to have known you and I am honored to see you grow up to be such a strong man like our father. However, no matter how high you rise or how big you get, you'll always be my Little Baby Brother.

To my sons, Baba loves you more than you will ever know until you have your own...as your Gran always told me. Thank you for making me the richest man in the world.

To Susan, Carol, Roy, Doe, Elizabeth, Genevieve, Adele, Ron, and Cindy, it was so hard settling and acclimating to life here in America at the beginning and even now, but you have helped and continue to help our family beyond explanation because you saw something in us. No words and thank-you's were, are, and will ever be enough, but thank you again and forevermore.

To everyone who contributed to make this book a reality, whether you know it or not, from the bottom of my heart, thank you.

To the sales reps who are struggling right now and the ones who know they could be doing better, if I can do it, you can do better.

Last, but not least, to my master, my mentor, my brother, and my dear friend, David "The Mentor to the Mentors" Corbin…aho.

Be on the look out...

Preface

For over half a year, I was in a really dark and bad place that I wouldn't wish upon my worst enemy. Got fired from my cushy job. Two businesses failed in epic fashion. Most of my life savings gone. And I was about to lose my house. I am still going through the legal breakup as I write this book. Massive debt, depression, anxiety attacks, and thoughts of suicide were my closest companions. I was crawling, on my hands and knees, at the bottom of the deepest, darkest pit of hell. Nothing tasted good. I found no enjoyment in life. I had shut myself off from the rest of the world, no social media, no phone calls, and definitely no get-togethers. My marriage was in shambles, to put it lightly. Only my kids brought a little bit of enjoyment, and even then, I was too lost in my own suffering to be fully present with them.

My father had finally had enough so he made a special trip in his busy schedule to come down to visit me in Long Beach from Northern California.

One night, during a conversation, I was crying to my dad, "Dad, I'm a failure, I've got nothing, I'm nothing, I'm zero! I'm sorry, Dad!"

For the second time in my life, my father yelled at me. The first one was in college, and for a variety of college related reasons which many of you will probably sympathize with.

"Son, you have no idea about zero! You are light years away from zero! Light years away from zero! Your mom and I started with real zero four times in our life! You haven't even gotten close to zero once! Not once! Let me tell you about zero! Your mom and I had zero when we got married after the war. We had zero when we had to flee Laos where you were born. We had zero when we got to Chieng Kham Refugee Camp in

Thailand. And we started with zero again for the last time when we came to America! We had zero red cents in our pockets. That's Zero!"

The tears started coming and my dad's heart broke again as it always does anytime one of his two sons cry. The two things in the world he cares about most in this life are his two sons. Seeing my tears, he lowered his voice.

"Son, zero is having nothing but the clothes on your back and having to start over in a brand new country."

He reached into his pocket, pulled out what amounted to less than 20 cents and said, "Zero is when we came to America with less money than the change I got in my pocket right now."

"Zero is not knowing any English in this country."

"Zero is having no idea of how we were going to take care of you and your brother...and your grandma and grandpa as well."

"Zero is not knowing any of the culture and customs of this country."

"Zero is not knowing how to drive."

"Zero is not having any education."

"Zero is not having any work experience."

"That's zero."

"You are light years away from zero, My Son."

"You know English very well, you know everything about this country, you have a couple of cars, you still have a house, a little bit left of your 401K, you have a college education, you have a lot of management experience, you were a great sales rep, you can find a job anytime as a sales rep with your friends or any company but you just don't want to work!"

He added, "And you don't even have to take care of your mom and I, like we did your grandma and grandpa. And we've been helping you out tremendously these last couple of years. Not only that, if you really need help, if you really lose everything...you can come live with us. And if not us, you have a brother, who is a doctor, and I'm sure he will let you and your family live with him. And not only that, you have in-laws in Canada who will let you live with them. And not only that, you have a brother-in-law in Canada as well who will let you guys live with him. And not only that, you've got so many cousins and friends, who I'm sure will let you guys live in their garage if you need to."

"We didn't have any of that when we came here! If your mom and I failed, then you, your brother, your grandma and grandpa, and all of us will be on the streets. That's real zero, Son."

All I could do was cry and say, I'm sorry. I was so very wrong and ungrateful. I realized I didn't have zero at all, my dad was right. I was light years away from zero. In fact, I was the richest man on the planet and I already had all the things a man could ever ask for: a wonderful wife, beautiful kids, the greatest family and friends, enough money to do what's important to me, massive opportunity, and freedom.

My dad really kicked my ass – what a real man needs to do when his kid deserves it. I had to let it soak in for a couple of weeks. Then slowly I started to come out of my hole as gratitude crept in and filled up the empty selfish space that was created by my own self-loathing, pity, and suffering.

The funny thing about gratitude is that it can always leave you if you're not careful. I used to be the most grateful person you'd ever meet until I started living in Los Angeles.

I was born and raised in the Refugee Camps in Thailand after the Vietnam War. The camps were in the middle of the jungle and in the middle of nowhere near the border of Thailand and Laos. We had nothing. I was eight when we came to America at the end of 1987 so I was old enough to know most of the hardships that we suffered through. There was no electricity, running water, flushing toilets, fridges, microwaves, dishwashers, washers and dryers, or almost anything else most people don't even blink an eye about here. The menu every single meal of every single day was dried sardines and rice. The United Nations would drop bags of the dried fish and rice off helicopters. The corrupt Thai guards with guns who didn't want to be there guarding a bunch of "savages" would take half the food and then distribute the other half to the ten thousand or so refugees they were guarding within the barb-wire fenced camp. Of course, being a kid, ration day was always a fun time for me. I loved going to line up with my dad and my grandpa. Each would carry a basket of dried sardines or rice home, with me skipping happily alongside them. The first two weeks were always great times because you may actually have full fillets of fish to eat at each meal. There was usually only one meal a day – grilled or stir-fried most of the time. But the last two weeks consisted mainly of fish-bone soup and rice because we would save all the heads and bones in a basket. That's when it really sucked and you have to get creative.

Creative was being able to sew, find a few odd jobs around the camp, make things, trade things, or any number of ways to work and save whatever you could. Once a year, maybe, if it was a good year, if your family was creative and could make some stuff happen to sell and trade, then you might get a chicken leg and a hard-boiled egg. That was always the greatest day of the year for me. First, I would crumble the hard-boiled egg, sprinkle on a little salt, and slowly suck on the bits until it melted and disappeared in my mouth. Then I would savor that chicken meat all day. After all the chicken meat was gone, I would crush the bone with my teeth, break open the marrow, and suck out every single bit of delicious marrow that I could. Then I'd crunch on the bone until it splintered into a thousand pieces and all the juices had been rung out, and the whole thing was completely obliterated. Man, those were the days. People used to ask me if I ever got sick of sardines. Hell, no. There was never enough of it for me to get sick of it.

It was only until I got to America, after suffering through years of ridicule, bullying, social and cultural expectations, media negativity, climbing the corporate ladder, early success, later failures, corporate America, and my own struggles that I started to believe I wasn't enough. That was when my gratitude turned to ungratefulness. That was when everything started going downhill. That was when the entitlement crept in. That was when blame and self-victimization took over responsibility. That was when belief gave way to fears, doubts, and excuses. That was when everything fell apart and I hit rock bottom and lived in a state of hell on earth.

Fortunately, even though gratitude could leave, it could also come back; albeit, normally it takes a good ass whoopin' of some mental or physical sort to get back this gratitude state. My dad gave me that ass whoopin' that I needed.

However, after the ass whoopin', it didn't fully click until a month or so later when my cousin, TC, and I were driving back one night from San Diego. TC said to me, "Hey, my little brother, BC, called me yesterday and we were talkin' and he was askin' me why is it that you don't come up anymore and talk to us about how to be successful like you used to?"

My reply was an uninspired, "Why the hell would anyone want to listen to me, I'm a freakin' goddamn failure!"

TC shot back quickly, "Yeah, but they don't know that, and they don't think that. In their eyes, you and your brother are the most successful people they know. And they want and need to hear from you because nobody else is gonna do it."

That one sentence my cousin said sealed the deal.

I told my cousin, "You're right, I need to man the hell up and start giving back. It's about damn time!"

I made a deal with him that I will no longer be selfish and scared anymore because massive failure has beaten the fear out of me. Now I will be successful and I will do so by giving back. So here it is.

But first, let me stop and say that this all happened because of Keng Yang. Rest in peace, Little Cousin, Little brother.

Keng Yang

I was fine until he woke up from his tired sleep to mutter, "You guys drive safe, ok?"

I turned to look back at him and saw my little cousin, Keng Yang, not even 21 years old, barely able to extend his tubed-up right arm, to wave a concerned goodbye to my brother and I as we were leaving. That image will stay with me for the rest of my life. Here my little cousin was, on his deathbed, slipping in and out of consciousness, barely able to drink, speak, or breathe, and he was concerned about our safety? Even though the sliding glass door wasn't even locked, I struggled to pull it open so I could hurry outside into the hallway. Only with desperate reluctance, I was able to hold back the flood of tears to only a few drops. Not being able to stand from all the shaking and dizziness, I leaned back against the cold, slick hospital wall and my knees collapsed, and I sank down to the floor with my face buried in my hands to hide the tears. My heart was broken and my soul was shattered to a depth I didn't know was possible. I didn't know it right there and then, but my life would never be the same again.

My younger brother drove up separately from Santa Barbara that Friday morning while I drove up from my house in Long Beach in Southern California. It took me almost seven hours in the car, daydreaming about various things like the actual condition of my cousin, my job which I hated, my relationship with my wife which was disastrous, my two awesome little boys and the silly things they do, golf which I used as an escape, and a whole lot about how and why my life didn't turn out exactly the way I had hoped it would. I never gave too much serious thought to each particular subject, however. My mind just wandered briefly through each like I practiced in real life.

That particular hospital in Sacramento was like any other stark, white-walled one I've ever been to. Once you've been to one hospital, you've been to them all. There was that familiar sanitary smell all around like someone mixed Mr. Clean and bleach, and slathered it all over everything. The only thing more pervasive was a serious, sad, and somber cloud that was invisible, yet tangible, heavy, and always looming. It took at least three pumps of sanitizer just to feel a bit less drenched in contamination so I could manage to navigate my way through the hallways.

I barely recognized my little cousin because he was so emaciated.

Keng woke up to say, "Hey Kao…" which made me well up inside, while amazed at how he even recognized me after all these years compounded by the fact that he was barely able breath or open his eyes. Even though my parents had called me to visit Keng because they said he may not have long to live, it was only then that I grasped the full imminent seriousness of his departure.

I asked Keng the usual and customary How Are You's and You Doin' OK's because I didn't know what else to say. I just told him that I was here, I miss him, I love him, and that we are all here for him so he needs to get better and come home. He nodded in agreement and then slipped back into a long sleep after that.

We had stayed there at the hospital in North Sacramento for a couple of hours talking to Keng's brothers and sisters, and our uncles. My oldest uncle talked the most to my brother and I, but Keng's father, my mom's second oldest brother, was so distraught and drained from the whole ordeal for weeks that he hardly acknowledged me, and barely spoke to my brother before going back to sleep on a little foldout bed brought in by the nurses. We stayed there and caught up with our cousins and their friends and significant others about the family and life in general.

Keng was the third youngest of my mom's youngest two brothers. Keng was such a good kid, a great kid in fact – fun-loving, light-hearted, always concerned for others, and everyone liked him. I knew him when he was just a little boy, before they moved down to Sacramento from Willows after I graduated from high school and went down to L.A. so I never saw him grow up after I moved out. I saw him a few times every couple of years at family gatherings of sorts, but never hung out or got to know him like my other cousins who were living up north in NorCal. Everyone loved him and for good reason – they said he was a kind, considerate, and strong person. When he was very young – I think about five or six years old, fully able to run and speak – he was playing around outside his apartment home, and he got hit by a car and was rolled over by the car. Because his family had only recently arrived from Thailand, they couldn't speak English so my mom was called to translate at the local Glenn Medical Hospital.

Mom tears up every single time she described this moment. She showed up worried, saw scared Little Keng, and all he could say was, "Auntie, my leg hurt, hurt so much, am I going to be okay?"

My mom said, "It's going to be okay, Little Keng, you're at the hospital now, they are going to take care of you just fine."

A sad but relieved Little Keng answered in the bravest and cutest voice, "Okay…"

The doctors said he had a broken leg, but because he was so young, surgery would not be needed. They said bracing, time, and medication will help him heal up. He made it out of that near fatal incident to thrive and bring happiness to everyone he touched.

Some of Keng's friends and family came one after another to see him, bringing food and gifts. I remember he got a few Jordan sneakers, everyone knew he loved sneakers. He used to post Facebook pictures of his new sneakers. They would shake him a little to wake him up just long enough for him to recognize them, then he would mutter in gratitude and appreciation before eventually quickly fading back into sleep. Many times, though, he would wake from his slumber to complain about the pain and the itchiness in his chest. Moaning and asking for drugs if he was conscious enough or he'd just feverishly scratch his chest, after which his oldest brother, Chou, would ask the nurse to turn up the IV medication and then take a wet cloth and reach under Keng's hospital gown to softly wipe his chest and stomach until the scratching subsided. I just sat there helpless, awkward, fidgeting, and passed the time by trying to make conversation with my cousins and the family.

Several hours passed and my brother and I were ready to leave as Keng's condition wasn't getting any better and we couldn't help very much. We said our goodbyes to the family and Chou agreed there wasn't anything we can do so we might as well go see our parents in Willows sooner as opposed to later, and he would call us if anything happened. So I rubbed Keng's head to wake him and told him we were leaving.

He woke at that point and said to me, "Hey Kao, thanks for coming. How's L.A.? I just wanna see L.A. one time before I die."

I told him that soon he will get better and come down to visit me in L.A., and I will show him around. My brother said goodbye to Keng in the same fashion and we turned towards the door to leave when Keng uttered the words that brought me down to my knees, "You guys drive safe, OK?"

On the way up to Willows – a small farming town about an hour and fifteen minutes north of Sacramento, straight up the I-5 Highway – right after passing the airport and the bridge over the main river, the full realization of Keng's situation hit me. Here was a good, young boy, who had never done anything bad to anyone, never even been anywhere outside of Northern California, never traveled, never seen the world, never even got laid I think, and all he wanted to do was see L.A., one time before he died, which I knew he would never, but here I was living down in L.A. for over fifteen years already. And just like that, the impact hit me like running full speed into a brick wall. There was no remorse or hesitation. Like a beaten, vengeful caged animal – seeing the perfect opportunity to pounce on me after years of abuse – it viciously and furiously overwhelmed me. An uncontrollable flood of tears erupted from every available orifice of my face, suffocating me. I couldn't breathe and was lucky to still be able to keep the car on the road as it was almost impossible to see through the tears and still manage to have the strength to hold the steering wheel straight.

It would be a couple of years before I realized that it was not anger that I felt, although it certainly felt like the most angry and shameful thing I'd ever experienced. I was angry at myself for forgetting why I went down to L.A. in the beginning. I was angry because I had forgotten all about my dream. I was angry at myself for beating my dream up, for pushing my dream down so deep, for sealing it in a dark underground dungeon, and for forgetting where I put the keys. I was even more angry at myself because I had given up on my dream entirely. However, much to my dismay, what I felt wasn't anger! What I felt was my dream rushing back stronger than ever. It had not given up on me. After all those years! As patiently as possible, it had been smoldering quietly in the dark, behind heavy closed doors, hoping and believing, slowly and faithfully building up the strength it needed to turn into a firestorm that would scorch the earth once I let it out.

Keng was here, then in six months he was gone. He started feeling tired at the beginning of 2013. As each day passed he grew more and more tired, showing up late to work or not at all. He told his parents, but they delayed taking him to the hospital in fear of paying medical bills because they didn't have insurance. It was only after losing his job at the Sacramento Airport did they finally take him to see a doctor. The doctor didn't see anything wrong and sent him back home. Then his condition worsened and they had no choice but to go back to see another doctor. That doctor referred Keng to a specialist in San Francisco who did some tests on him. After another month, they got the results back and he was already stage 4 cancer of the esophagus; a rare cancer, apparently. They were told that he only had months left to live. When everyone finally accepted his fate and I got the call about his situation, it would only be one month before he passed in the fall.

My brother and I stayed with my parents on Friday and Saturday night. Obviously, the mood was very somber and my brother and I talked with my parents quite a bit on the sofa about what a shame it was to be losing such a young good-hearted soul. My mom kept saying what a poor boy Keng was to have suffered so much when he was young when he got ran over by that car, only to meet his end like this at still such a young age. There was a lot of kissing and holding hands from my mom while my dad stayed the quiet and thoughtful person he normally is, maybe saying a word or two in agreement with Mom. My mom called at least once a day to check on the status of Keng and got at least one call from my oldest uncle, Chou, or one of her nieces regarding the status. From that we knew his health was fading fast and his time on earth was coming to an end. The doctor had informed them that it would only be a matter of days and could be anytime. Then we left on Sunday morning around 9 A.M. to go check on Keng one last time, before heading home on that familiar long drive back on The 5.

The 5. Interstate-5. I-5. Over a thousand miles of open road starting at the border of Mexico straight up through middle of California and all the way to the border of Canada. You'll see mostly only hills and mountains in the distance, some tumbleweeds, cows pastoring in open plains, gas stations, fruit stands, farms, rice fields, towns so small you'll pass them by if you blink, and an occasional capital of the state. You don't know how large California truly is until you've driven through it on The 5. I love it all. Over on the left, on the coast, is the Pacific Ocean…one of a kind. Over on the right are the majestic Sierras. In the middle is Central California, the agricultural capital of the world. Up top is Northern California, constantly trying to secede from the South, a place I love and hate. And then there's sunny Southern California, my favorite place in the world, where dreams come true or they go to die. I've spent countless hours on The 5.

Again, the same hospital feel and the same sanitary atmosphere. This time Keng wasn't even conscious. My brother and I both knew he will never open his eyes again. We both stayed for about an hour and a half, but this time the mood was not conversational. Everyone's eyes were red and swollen from all the crying. I remember thinking to myself, that it must have been because of only two reasons why there were no tears, it was either all cried out, or everyone had finally accepted the inevitable. Then Chou came up to let us know that there's nothing we can do and we've got a long drive ahead of us so we better get going before it gets too late. With reluctant agreement, we hugged Chou and the rest of the family, and said our last goodbyes to Keng. I just kissed him on the forehead and told him I love him and to get better so he can come see me in L.A soon. My brother did the same and we sadly walked through the hospital back out, and down to our cars. We said our careful goodbyes, hugged each other, sighed, got in our cars, and drove off and onto The 5 South. As I pulled slowly away, I raised my hand to signal a peace sign to the rear-view mirror back to my brother and to Keng, and watched as they both disappeared amidst the cars, buildings, and trees – knowing full well that I'd only see one of my brothers ever again.

On the long eight-hour drive back from Sacramento to my house in Long Beach, all I kept thinking of was Keng, why this happened, and how unfair life was. I experienced the whole gamut of emotions and feelings. From anger towards his parents for their ignorance, to anger for the incompetence of the doctors, to regret that I never got to know him well, to self-pity for my own jaded, defeated, and cynical view of life, and to self-hatred for taking for granted living down in L.A. for so long and forgetting what it was like the first time I went down there to visit. I had forgotten all about the feeling of awe, hope, and inspiration I experienced upon arriving in L.A.

Then something strange happened. About 15 minutes before the Grapevine, right before The 99 and The 5 joined, as I saw the mountain range approaching, I began to feel excited, surreal, and powerful about getting away from NorCal. I saw L.A. behind the mountains. I saw a vision of me chasing my dreams and conquering the world. It felt familiar…déjà vu.

This felt exactly like the time I moved down to Long Beach to go to college. It was special. We came to this very same Grapevine point at the end of August 1998, on my way to the dorms at Long Beach State for my first semester in college, in my White Toyota Tacoma truck with oversized wheels that would always scrape the side of the wheel arch every time I try to make a wide turn. The bed was lightly loaded with everything I owned which was nothing more than a pillow, a fluffy peacock-decorated Chinese blanket, a small mini fridge, a 13" TV/VCR Combo, a compact stereo boom-box, a large luggage filled with clothes, hangars, and shoes, some posters of Bruce Lee, and a black plastic tarp tightly covering the entire bed. Sometimes I would sit back and wish again to be able to pack all my belongings in less than an hour into the back of a car and just go anywhere…oh, what I would give. My parents came with me to drop their excited young man off to college while my mom tried to hold back her tears the whole way down. She gave me the longest, hardest hug and kiss goodbye after we quickly unloaded everything into my dorm room. I was ready and excited to go meet all my new friends. My mom would later reminisce that I was in such a rush to turn around and run back to meet my new friends that I never even turned around to see my mom crying out of control while my dad yelled at her to be strong and not let me see her cry. I never even gave it a thought.

I knew that beyond those mountains was L.A., beyond those mountains were my dreams about to be realized, and beyond those mountains was my destiny. My heart started pounding harder and harder in my chest and my breathing became more rapid. Long Beach, L.A., Southern California, and all these wonderful and amazing things and people were waiting for me, and all I had to do was get there, explore it, and take whatever I wanted. Everything was there – my hopes, my dreams, my future, the culmination of my prior successes, and the anticipation of future successes and riches were almost in reach. I was confident that nothing was going to stop me. There was not a shred of fear, only uncontainable ambition and power. I was all in on my dreams.

That was the same feeling I felt. It brought back further familiar feelings and excitement from my young days in L.A.

I had the world in the palm of my hands.

And nothing will ever stop me again.

Why did I tell you that story?

Because I want everyone to know that Keng did not pass away for nothing. He lived long enough to make a difference in my life. He lived long enough to change my life forever. He gave me the courage, strength, and belief in myself again so I can inspire others to live the life that they have dreamed of too. I promise you, Keng didn't die for nothing. I WILL make him live forever. He will never be forgotten because I will share his story with everyone I encounter so that they remember his name and everyone will know how he impacted my life, and find inspiration in their own lives.

Keng showed me that life is short and nobody knows what the future will hold or how much time you have, so you might as well go out there and do whatever you want, whatever it is. Obviously, I'm only advocating legal things here. I don't care how stupid it sounds to everyone, and I don't care how stupid it sounds to even yourself at the moment. It doesn't matter what anyone says. What I am doing right now, is living proof of that. What you are reading right now is a testament to the life I dreamed about but never believed possible. A couple of years ago, if you were to tell me that in two years I would be rich beyond my wildest dreams, have the luckiest, most beautiful family and friends, be an author, sales trainer, motivational speaker, get to work out every single day, draw, paint, golf, enjoy quality time with my family, travel, eat a massive amount of Pho' noodles, and do everything I ever wanted to do every single day of my life, I would say you were crazy. But because of Keng, I am living my dreams and my passions. My sincerest hope is that because of him, you will too, and in doing so, help me make my cousin live forever.

Before we continue though, I want to let you know that you don't have to have someone you know die too young or be touched by the proximity of death before you take action. You don't have to learn things the hard way. You don't have to make mistakes yourself personally before learning difficult lessons so please learn from me, my story, and from what I will share in this book. Furthermore, everything I will share with you, you already know. You already have within you everything it takes to succeed in life and in every other area of your life. However, sometimes we all forget our dreams, lose ourselves, lose our way, let life and people beat us up, and take for granted all the miracles we have right in front of us, which are family, friends, food, love, and life. Finally, the purpose of this book is to remind you of the power, duty, and opportunity that you have within you to be successful beyond your wildest dreams.

Introduction

This book is about what it takes to beat the odds in sales and in any area of your life. I believe that sales is what makes the world go round. Every day and in every relationship, you are selling, whether you like it or not. You're fooling yourself if you think you're not selling in any situation, whether consciously or subconsciously. The ones who are the best at salesmanship get the results they are looking for. That's how you make new friends, how you get a job, how you get promoted, how you get the girl or guy, how you win in life, how you stay in business, how you get the sale, or just about anything else. You may have the best idea, product, or technology in the world, but if you can't sell it, then it's not going to do anyone any good. In addition, you're going to be out of business sooner or later if you've got no sales coming in. I learned this the hard way many times.

As the old saying goes, "Sales cures all problems." If you don't believe this, remember me when your sales start to go down. Worse yet, wait till your sales keep going down. No matter how good of a person you are, how well-liked you are, how great your methods are, you're going to have to answer for it. You may be asked by your company to work a lot harder, log a lot more sales calls in your CRM program to prove you're not just slacking off, work nights and weekends providing a detailed schedule of planned activities to your supervisor, or spend countless hours trying to provide chart after chart after chart of data to show why you're not hitting your numbers and what you plan to do to correct it. Some unfortunate souls will be put on some sort corrective action plan to get back to budget. The very unlucky and unable will face termination.

This is what I call the Sales Pit.

It's a deep, dark, dreary, and lonely place and it takes a lot out of you mentally and physically to claw yourself out of it. Some might be tempted to clean up their LinkedIn profiles and resumes just in case things don't work out.

No matter how great your product performs, how inexpensive your product is compared to the competition, how great your marketing and email campaigns are, or how tight of a ship you run, or how wonderful of a personality you have, you will find out how bad things will turn out if sales keep staying down.

Anyone who's ever been here knows it's no fun at all, at work or at home.

Because I've been in the Sales Pit, these days I'd much rather be on the other side where the sales are healthy, the budgets are getting beat, the bosses are not hounding you, and you have plenty of time for customer entertainment, some golf, a few beers, and the sun is always shining bright. That's how it always seems to me anyway when I'm rolling. More importantly, the wife is happy because the bonuses and free vacations on the company are plenty.

Sales is everything.

Obviously, it is the best way to generate revenues. The best method is to hire and keep training an awesome team of highly skilled sales specialists to effectively communicate all your company's products and services to meet the customers' needs. Your sales people are the ones who deal with the customer the most, they're out in the trenches every day, have the best relationships with the customers, and can provide the best product, service, pricing, quality assurance, operations, logistics, and feedback to the company for further opportunities, improvements, and continued sales revenue growth. You need sales and you need to develop a culture within your organization that has what I call the All-In Factor. Sales is a numbers game and sometimes the odds in those numbers seem almost insurmountable, unless you have the All-In Factor. The All-In Factor is the mindset and skills you need to overcome any odds stacked against you. This book is about how to overcome those odds.

If you picked up this book, you're either a sales person who actually cares about your station in life or you are a decision-maker in your company that wants to improve sales for the welfare and future of everyone in your organization. The reason you'll enjoy this book is because if I can do it, then anyone can. I overcame the most incredible odds to become one of the best sales people in my industry and lived to tell about it. In this book, I will chronicle some of the ways in which I was able to overcome those odds and accomplish my American Dream and beyond, and how you can do it too. I will also share some very basic, fundamental truths and strategies about sales that you or any organization can utilize to turn you and your organization into a top-notch sales machine. And don't worry, I assure you the methods I'm about to share with you is not that complicated. Anyone can use them. That's the real genius of it all. I'm not that smart and it worked for me. That means it is definitely going to work for you. You just have to be All In. In this book, I'll show you how simple it is to be All In. However, simple and easy are two very different things.

Sales is hard, make no doubt about it. Sales is hard for most people and deathly hard for some, like me when I first started. In fact, according to most personality and behavioral tests, I should never have been a sales rep. I probably should have been an CPA, an artist, or an engineer in a lab somewhere. Truth be told; few are natural born sales people, and because of that, they usually take their gifts for granted like many of my tall, good-looking, and likeable friends who've never had to struggle as a sales rep. Those guys have never had to hustle for anything they've wanted – much less having to hustle just to survive like I did – so they never had to push their own boundaries and, therefore, will never live up to their full potential. But I didn't write this book for them anyway. They really don't need it because they are usually living in the excellent "A" range of sales and life, from pure talent and upbringing. Those types of people will always do fine and any organization is lucky to have them. They may find this book too "simple", too "basic", too "fundamental", or too "beneath them." However, if they do happen to pick this book up, they may find that these fundamentals that I'm about to share will never go away and may give them a great refresher and maybe just a nudge to be "A+" or "Legendary" status.

The best pros all make it look so easy and effortless. What most people don't know or refuse to believe is that the pros have mastered the basic fundamentals, that is why it looks so effortless. This is true of all art forms, studies, professions, crafts, and disciplines. Michael Jordan, Bruce Lee, Tiger Woods, Wayne Gretzky, Picasso, Muhammad Ali, Roger Federer, The Beatles, Steve Jobs, Bill Gates, Warren Buffett, John D. Rockefeller, Jim Rohn, Zig Ziglar, Brian Tracy, Tony Robbins, or anyone else in history who is considered great have all mastered the fundamentals. Even if you are already living and operating in the excellent "A" range of sales or life, you will find something useful or appreciate the "reminder" fundamentals that I will be sharing. Who knows, this might even catapult you into the Greatest of All Time discussion.

Then there's the rest of us who are either above average, average, below average, or failing at sales and in life. This book will give you the mindset and fundamentals it takes to go from any failing or average range and push you up to the excellent range like I was able to do. Let me tell you, I was probably the worst sales rep in the history of mankind. No lie. It was bad; really, really bad, in fact. I will illustrate further in the coming chapters how bad. If you sucked or am sucking as a sales rep right now, you'll get a kick out of my pain and struggle, and hopefully, should you choose to apply yourself, you'll be a lot better for it.

For the most part, average people underestimate the fundamentals and that is why they are average. It's not because they lack some natural genius or skill, it's that they just lack some basic beliefs and some basic understanding of what it takes to be successful because they've just never done it before and most importantly, have never done what it takes to get there so they believe it's impossible. I have seen this in myself and in most people across all areas of life such as sports, fitness, work, marriage, kids, management, business, sales, and just about anything else. In their quest to hurry up, get better, get advanced, and do well, they usually neglect form, footwork, safety, rules, values, gratitude, and other fundamentals that are necessary to get them there. Then they get stuck when the odds are stacked against them. Oh, and I promise you, the odds will keep on stacking. Everyone gets stuck at some point or another at anything they do. It never gets easier as you get older. Most people at this point will start to rely on old habits to carry them through instead of a set of fundamental principles to systematically get better and beat the odds. Luckily for you, I will give you these principles in this book.

But like anything, knowing will not get you results, you've got to practice what you know. And you can't just use it once. Doing anything once will never make you good at anything. You've got to use it for at least 3 months to several years, every single day, consecutively, until it becomes a winning habit. That's why I love the P90X workout products you see on late nights at 3 in the morning – because from personal experience, it really works if you spend 90 days doing the workouts as intended. Forget those 21 day diets or overnight "secrets." Here's the real secret: there is no secret! That's probably why some of you have been failing. It's because you think it's a secret. The only real secret is that it was within you all along to begin with if you would just take the time to coax it out of yourself. It takes a special person to be a great sales person. The good news is that you are already special and you can do it. But it's going to take everything you got and more…you're going to have to be All In. In this book, I will show you how I was able to beat the odds in sales and give you some fundamental principles you must master in order to succeed at the highest levels of sales and more importantly, in life.

I am the best example I know of beating the odds. How do you beat the odds when you were born in a refugee camp after spending most of your young, impressionable years in it? You don't, unless you happen to learn how to defeat that which you were born into and beat the odds that every one of your cousins and people you know couldn't.

How do you come to America – not knowing simple stuff like ABC – when you were eight years old, and in 10 years become valedictorian of your high school. Only less than 1% of natural born English speakers can do that. How do you come from such ingrained poverty mentality and become wealthy beyond your imagination? Not even most of the people who were born here in America with all the information and opportunities available to them could do that. How do you come from the jungles of Laos and Thailand, after the Vietnam War, to not just survive, but to successfully thrive in the suburbs of Los Angeles? How do you survive on a basket of dried sardines and rice every month for 8 years of your young life to eating anything you want in America? Nowadays, the hardest question is, what restaurant to choose from tonight. How do you become the number one basketball player on your high school team being 5'3" tall? (I grew up to be 5'5" and a ½" by the way). How do you become the number one tennis player on your high school team not knowing how to serve and picking up tennis only when you got to high school? How do you graduate college when you're the very first of your whole line of ancestors to attend college? How do you become a top performing manager when you and your people couldn't look at a single white person in the eye? How do you marry and stay married outside your race when you're the first one to do in the history of your whole family? How do you become a top performing sales rep when you have such a distinct, deathly fear of talking to people, literally slapped into your subconscious by your grandpa? The odds were stacked against me. Most people would have quit a long time ago or found another more "suitable" occupation and lifestyle. Ladies and Gentlemen, I'm about to tell you how to beat the odds in sales and in life.

Being great at sales, successful at any endeavor, fulfilling your dreams, accomplishing your goals, and living your passions all require some fundamental truths. I've boiled these truths into 4 simple steps with examples, anecdotes, and reflections from my own life to illustrate that if I can do it, anyone can. These same 4 simple steps that I will explain can be used to accomplish anything you want in life.

Again, I must be truthful in letting you know that even though it is easy to follow and simple in nature, it is quite hard in practice, otherwise you probably wouldn't be reading this book. Simple and easy are two very different things. Do not confuse the two like I once did. It will probably take more than you've ever had, more than you've ever given, and more than who you are right now, but I promise you, you have it within you, however deep you must dig to find it, it is there. It may take months, years, or even a lifetime to accomplish your goals, depending on how big you make them. It's very simple, but it's not easy. Just like losing weight, it's actually very simple to lose weight. Essentially, it's just calories in versus calories out. If you burn more calories than you take in, over an extended period, you will be skinnier. That's it, fact! It's actually very simple, but it's not easy. I want to make sure this is understood before we go forward.

I will share with you these simple truths, fundamental principles, life lessons, and practical tips on how I was able to get it done. You may need to apply all of them like I had to, or you may need to use only one or two to allow you to break on through to the success you've always sought. If you can't use it now, my hope is that you can use it later. If you know someone who can use this, please help me share it with them so that they may have the opportunity to be successful, give back, and share the story of my little cousin, Keng Yang. If I can do it, I know you can do it!

I want to make one thing very clear before we begin. You don't need this. Nobody needs this. There's nothing wrong with you. I'm not trying to change you. You are fine just the way you are. You are still loved. Even if you don't take anything from this book, trust me, the sun will still shine tomorrow, and life will go on. Make no doubt about it. If there's one thing I have learned about life is that life is what you make of it. On the other hand, if you want to stop suffering, if you want to do better than just fine, if you want to take care of your family the way they deserve, if you want to leave a worthy legacy, if you want to be an example, if you want to be something, if you want to make a difference to yourself and others, if you want to chase down your dreams, if you want to be great, if you want to explore the limits of your potential, if you want to be successful beyond your wildest dreams, if you want to be the best damn sales machine that ever lived, and if you want to do something truly extraordinary in life, then you will want to take some notes.

Step One: Believe in Yourself

"The Only Belief That Matters is Self-Belief" — Anonymous

Chapter 1: All In

"You don't want to go to America, Boy! When you step off the plane, white demons will pick you up with chopsticks, stir-fry you, and wash you down with wine!"

That's what my grandparents would always tell me when I was a young boy living in the refugee camps in Thailand. The refugee camp was where I was born and raised for almost 8 years. It was a place in the middle of nowhere, away from civilization, where the UN threw a bunch of tents and warehouses together surrounded by barb wired fence, with iffy water and sewage systems, and where they put thousands of refugees. Refugees are people like me who didn't have a country, usually because of the results of war. Every day the menu consisted of dried sardines and rice that the UN would drop off helicopters and the Thai guards would take half the food and ration the rest to the 10,000 plus refugees living in captivity. Our camp was called Chieng Kham Refugee Camp and it was located near the Laos/Thailand border like most camps in the aftermath of the Vietnam War – safe from the retaliation of Laos and Vietnam, but also safely tucked away from Thai civilization. My grandparents didn't want to go to America because life in the jungles, mountains, and refugee camps were all they ever knew. Even though all they've ever experienced were hard-living, war, hunger, poverty, death, and tragedy, it was normal and comfortable to them, and they were fine with that.

Through the usual old-people gossip, my grandparents heard of many horror stories about the elders who've gone to the United States before them and sent audio cassette tape recordings back to them warning that in the new country they would be dependent on little kids to go anywhere or do anything because they can't speak English and don't know any of the culture or customs of America. The thought of complete

36

dependence and becoming the lowest caste members of this new society was utterly and completely frightening to them. All their lives in the old country, they were the wisest and most respected. Nothing important gets done without their approval – birth, marriage, New Year celebration, funerals, law and order, or any other important ceremony and ritual. Without a written language, all our knowledge was passed down verbally through the elders and through our distinct and intricate embroideries. I used to overhear the old people gossip in disgust at the thought of begging a little child to take them to buy food at the market because they can't make change. Even though they were fully aware of the many riches and opportunities available to them in America, this new world was just too new and too different from what they've always known. Thus, my grandparents would tell my brother and I of the "White Demons" every time they got the chance in the hope that we would be scared, somehow convince my parents, and tilt the favor to stay in Thailand. They were probably hoping that the vote would be four to two and that might sway my parent's decision about going to America. They had no chance because my parents were ALL IN on going to America and providing a real opportunity at a happy life for their two boys.

For our part in allying with the CIA and the U.S. during the Vietnam War, Hmong people were forced to fend for ourselves, flee for our lives, and survive on our own for over a decade after America pulled out in 1975. The lucky ones were able to escape Laos and Vietnam, avoid capture, avoid getting shot, avoid getting blown up by landmines, avoid drowning in the crossing of the heavily guarded Mekong River, make it to the Thai Refugee Camps, and endured life in captivity until they were sponsored to come to the U.S. We had to wait a very long time to be sponsored by the few Hmong on the front lines who were able to make it out immediately after the Fall of Saigon. Those officers and their families who were lucky enough and close enough to make it to the evacuation area were flown to

37

the U.S. or other allied countries such as France and Australia. They were sponsored by various angel church and non-profit organizations so that they could start a new life in their new country. After a few years of settling, they would be able to apply to sponsor their surviving extended families in the refugee camps in Thailand and those in turn would be able to do so later. It was an extremely slow and arduous process, a journey that would take over 30 years until most Hmong people were able to make it to America; sadly though, many never made it. Our family was the fourth and largest wave of refugees that were able to make it to America in the late 80's. My aunt married into a family in my camp who came in the 3rd wave in the early 80's, who had family that came in the second wave in the late 70's, who had family that was lucky enough to be near the evacuation zone and made it out during the first chaotic wave after the end of the Secret War.

1987 was a time of mass immigration to the United States for my people. Due to protests by Hmongs and people sympathetic to our plight here in America during the 80's, around 50,000 plus admissions were granted by the U.S. government to allow the majority of us to come here. Even as a young boy with absolutely no knowledge of the outside world, I could feel the hope in the air amidst the energetic commotion in the camp. All the men got together and decided that they didn't need all the Thai Badt money anymore because they couldn't use it in the United States. With the combined life savings from most of my relatives, they threw a big party to celebrate, and bought a table full of Pepsi, Sprite, 7-Up, and Orange Soda. Of course, being the paternal society that we were, only the men were invited. No women and children. Except for me, because I would always follow my dad where ever he went as all little boys across the world like to do.

As it were, they had their party in the southwest corner of the camp, next to the Red Cross nurses station. My dad saw me and yelled at me to go home but my uncle said I could stay because I was already there. He handed me a cup of this dark, black, bubbly liquid and I took my first sip of Pepsi. It was the most delicious, wonderful, and incredible thing I've ever tasted in my life! It was so sweet and tasty, sizzled, and it burned my throat! I said, this has to be the drink of the Gods sent down from the heavens to me! That was the singular most powerful experience of my entire life. Nothing has ever compared to that feeling again. I made up my mind that my life's goal was to drink as much Pepsi as possible.

The first time I ever drank Pepsi (Hmong people call every soda Peh'si). This was one of the only pictures we had in our possession so upon coming to the US, my dad needed an ID for school so he cut it

Coincidentally or not, about that time, my grandma and grandpa were lying to me vehemently about being stir-fried by white demons. Most of my life, I wondered why they would say such a thing to an impressionable young boy. It took me a very long time to find out the answer. It wasn't a coincidence at all. Even though all they knew in the old country was tragedy, poverty, and suffering, they would still rather hang on to the familiar than face the unknown, regardless if the unknown, America, was a real chance at happiness. This was the greatest lesson I've ever learned about the power of fear.

I was so scared, I went crying to my dad and said, "Dad, Dad, Grandma and Grandpa said if we go to America I'm going to get stir-fried by white demons and they're going to eat me while they drink wine! I don't want to get stir-fried, Dad! I don't want go to America!"

My dad then showed me a post card of New York City at night that he got from one of the French nurses at the camp hospital where he worked as a cafeteria cook. It was the first actual photo I've ever seen in my life. There were so many bright lights and tall silhouettes of countless, impossible buildings that it seemed like mountains of gold shimmering at night. My dad told me, "Son, look at this picture, this is America! If we go to America, you will get to live in palaces of gold just like this, and you'll have so much money, you can take showers in Pepsi every day."

To a kid who's never seen electricity before and was forever in love with Pepsi, that was all I needed to hear. I was SOLD. I told my dad, "Dad, I'm fast, I can out-run those white demons. I don't care what it takes, I'm going to take showers in Pepsi in America!"

It took almost a year after that before we got to America. We had to first get processed at the Phanat Nikhom Refugee Processing Center in Thailand. I hope you or anyone you know will never have to get processed in any way shape or form, because it could be an excruciating experience.

Leaving to a new Land

I remember leaving Chieng Kham Refugee Camp. There were so many people getting crammed into buses with nothing but what you can carry on your person, amidst the suffocating cries of uncertain goodbyes. There was a sea of crying family members left behind who were reaching up to the family members going, through bus windows, holdings hands, crying in sorrow, and not wanting to let go until the very last possible minute. People were throwing up left and right because they've never been on vehicles of any type, and most had severe motion sickness from the long bumpy ride all day on dirt roads. We arrived in the dead of night to the processing center. All I remember was pushing, pulling, scurrying, marching, flash lights, fireflies, or both, and desperately trying to hold my dad's hands in the pitch black endless chaos. Somehow, we hurried up just to be crammed like cattle in dusty warehouses waiting to get registered into the camp the next day or days, by the hundreds or thousands…a recurring nightmare that still haunts me to this day. After being registered, we rushed to settle and rest in our crammed warehouse along with many other families where we lived for about a year until we were processed and allowed to go to America. The floor was dirt and thin cloths or blankets were our beds. Walls separating each family were made of a simple thin cloth hung on a string across the long narrow warehouse, with up to 10 families in each warehouse. Growing up I still don't know how so many babies were made during this time because there were no privacy, walls, doors, or locks whatsoever.

Processing meant getting all the required health checks, learning English language and culture schooling, getting all the proper required registration papers completed, and getting small pox immunization shots on your arm that many of us immigrants call "FOB shots" (Fresh Off the Boat) which leave a dime sized "FOB mark" scar on your deltoid. The needles on those syringes were so big and long that it made most Hmong people deathly afraid of needles forevermore. No pain I've ever felt since has hurt more than those damn shots…perhaps it was the first time any of us has ever been exposed to a syringe and it happened to be a humongous one welded by the most crudely trained, indifferent Thai officials. But what choice did we have? I remember my parents and nurses holding me down while they plunged the needles into my left shoulder and I screamed out in pain and terror. My brother and several of my cousins never recovered from the fear of needles.

Registration also took a long time because nobody ever had birth or marriage certificates or any paperwork of any kind where we came from, and you're going to need those things in America as I would later come to find out. Unfortunately, for many, it would take many years if they had health complications or diseases. Every day my parents would lament to my uncles and aunts about the fact that someone they know had some health issues which would delay he or she going to America. I also heard many cases of people killing themselves because they would have to be turned back and forever barred from entering America because of some health issue. We were truly lucky and blessed to have been free from any big health issues. When I got older, I asked my dad if there were truly a lot of people who got turned back, and he said there were so many, it was almost like rolling the die each time you got a check-up. I thank God everyday someone was looking out for us.

We were also taught English and culture, or the semblance of it anyway. The Thai workers tried to teach the teens and adults, but the young ones like me and the elders didn't learn a damn thing. What we were taught probably wasn't even worth learning. They probably didn't believe we were smart enough to learn anything "complicated." They simply packed all the kids regardless of age into classrooms and taught the same lessons to everyone. The math we were taught was so simplistic and beyond patronizing. For God Sakes, it's just math! I distinctly remember being so proud of myself for being one of the fastest and best math students in the classroom. However, when we got to America, in the 3rd grade, I was the absolute worst math student ever. After failing every single math quiz – I mean badly, less than 50% correct, red marks on at least half the page – the teacher came and asked me to show her exactly how I was doing it. I proceeded to demonstrate to her by doing my math from left to right. Obviously, if you add from left to right, when the numbers have to be carried over, you are automatically wrong!

Example:

$$
\begin{array}{r}
56 \\
+ \quad 55 \\
\hline
= \quad 1011
\end{array}
$$

This is how I would normally add, multiply, or subtract. We were never taught any division as far as I can remember. I would just add the first numbers on the left column then the numbers on the right and be done with it. Nobody ever bothered showing me how to proof it. But when you're usually taught using small numbers only that don't need to be carried over, you can do it left-to-right or right-to-left and it would still be correct.

Example:

In fact, I was quite proficient at doing math this way because I was always the first one done, even in America. To this day, whatever the camps ingrained in me, I still initially look at every single math problem left to right then correct myself and go right to left. Obviously, a thinking person would scratch his head as to how I acquired such an abysmal skill. Maybe the teacher we were given was no smarter than a first grader. Perhaps nobody cared about what I learned and did not learn, survival was more important. Whatever the case, I learned it because the camp taught me such simple mathematics. This was just an example of the dysfunctional nature of the whole environment we were in at the time. America couldn't come soon enough.

At last, we finally landed at San Francisco International Airport in December of 1987, where much to my relief, I didn't see any giant white demons with chopsticks attempting to stir fry me, but I did see white ladies in black pantyhose and black ladies in white pantyhose while walking to our connection and thought to myself, "Wow, America is wonderful! White women have black legs and black women have white legs!"

We took another flight to Fresno Yosemite Airport where my aunt picked us up and drove us to her family's apartment in Visalia, California. While everyone was still vomiting from motion sickness since they've never been in car before, or as my grandma called it, "Big Shaky Box with Wheels," I immediately asked my aunt where the shower was and she pointed me to the bathroom. I ran in excited as I've ever been. After a while, I figured out how to turn on the shower, but much to my disappointment...no Pepsi came out at all...only water.

I came out crying to my Dad and said, "Dad, you lied to me, there's no Pepsi in the showers, you can't take showers in Pepsi in America!"

He told me, "Son, I didn't say Pepsi was free, you can still take showers in Pepsi, you just have to work for it. You have to do well in school, be smart, get a really good job, and make lots of money so that you can take showers in Pepsi!"

Sold! My first lesson in sales – find the man's motivation then you can sell him anything. Right there and then, I made up my mind I was going to be all in on my dreams of being so wealthy that I can take showers in Pepsi every day.

I've been *ALL IN* on chasing my Pepsi Dream ever since.

Chapter 1 #Truths

- To survive in a literal or figurative refugee camp, you must be All In on your dreams
- Find what your Pepsi Dream is and do whatever it takes to achieve it
- Sometimes white demons are just the ones you made up
- Pepsi doesn't just come out of the showers by itself
- Find the person's motivation then you can sell him anything.

Chapter 2: Coming to America

Our first month in America with my aunt's family

Our first five months in Visalia, California were both fantastic and traumatic. My parents were able to get Welfare benefits quickly so we moved into a small two-bedroom apartment not far from my aunt, with whom we lived with for a couple of months until we got settled. It was our very first real home that didn't have twigs, leaves, bamboo, or tin plates as part of the structure. My grandparents slept in one room while the four of us – my parents and my little brother and I – slept together on a thin mattress on the ground. This place was where I was able to finally learn how to ride a bike! I remember my uncle Chou Yee was the first Hmong person to own a bike when we were at the Refugee Processing Center. All the men and especially the boys thought he was a god.

My brother and I attended the closest elementary school, which was still across town. When winter break was over and everyone went back to school for the spring semester, I was enrolled in the 3rd grade and my brother was enrolled in kindergarten. The scariest moment my parents ever had was the first day of school in America. My parents, grandparents, and my aunt walked my brother and I about 3 blocks to the bus stop at the local intermediate school where we were picked up and dropped off at the elementary school. My aunt came along to show everyone where and when to drop us off as well as to pick us up after school. It was simple to everyone except my brother. Getting to school was no problem, but after school, my brother got off at the very first stop along with several other kids who were getting off. My parents waited and waited but he never arrived. I got out of school later so when they saw he wasn't with me and the buses stopped coming, they panicked. They called my aunt and everyone drove around town aimlessly for hours looking for my brother.

My brother – lost, scared, and confused – walked around crying with his shirt soaked from tears and his pants wet from peeing himself. Miraculously, a relative of my aunt's husband happened to see my five-year old brother crying on a random street while he was driving by. She stopped and asked my brother who his parents were, and luckily was able to decipher that my brother was from the new family that arrived in town from Thailand. She guessed that we were related to my aunt so she called my aunt and brought my brother back to us safely. It was a big town and my parents always thanked God that he wasn't kidnapped or lost forever. Welcome to the United States of America.

While my dad looked for any odd manual labor jobs that he could find like dishwasher and under-the-table construction jobs to help the family, my mom and my auntie went to adult school. Dad was 31 years old and Mom was 28 at the time. Strangers in a new world. Zero everything. All the while trying their darndest best to raise a family.

My mom was riding her bicycle one day to school and she got hit by a car trying to make a right at a corner. She was so ignorant and scared that she thought she was the one in trouble. In pain, she got up, apologized profusely to the Caucasian driver in her Hmong language, and limped off with her bike. The bike was so bent out of shape that she couldn't even ride it. When she finally got home, she was all bruised and bloodied with cuts and scrapes, but nobody knew what to do so we stayed quiet with angst hoping the driver somehow wouldn't call the police and have her arrested.

I had my first bad experience in America around Easter time. Our class was supposed to have a party and all the kids had to bring something to share with everyone. I volunteered when the teacher called out for someone to bring "Chocolate Eggs". Unfortunately, I didn't know the word "chocolate", I only knew "egg". Excited at the opportunity to make myself useful for the first time in America, I went home, asked my parents to take me to the grocery store so we could buy two dozen eggs, and proudly boiled them all for the next day's party. The following day, Grandma walked with my brother and I to the bus stop, with me happily carrying my large plastic bag filled with 24 carefully hard-boiled eggs. At the bus stop, a young Hmong girl in my classroom came up to me and asked if I had my chocolate eggs. I showed her the eggs and she erupted into laughter and proceeded to mock me, "You're stupid! You were supposed to get "Chocolate" eggs for our Easter party, but you're so stupid you brought regular eggs! You're the most stupid boy ever!" In shock and shame, I gave the eggs to my grandma to take home and sadly went to school empty-handed. I didn't say anything when the teacher asked me where the eggs were. I just sat quietly in the corner of the room all day, not speaking to anyone, holding the tears of shame back, and vowing never to be called stupid again. Another lesson learned – ignorance is no excuse.

Towards the end of spring 1988, one of my uncles found a one-month-free-rent deal up in Northern California, in a little small farming town called Willows, California. Just like that the majority of our relatives swarmed up there during that summer and others soon followed. The apartment complex was called Pineridge Apartments, and Willows was in for a rude awakening. It was a time of mass Hmong immigration from the refugee camps in Thailand to Central California, but due to Pineridge Apartments' rent deal, it was a time of mass Hmong migration from Central California to Northern California. Hmong people stick together. My grandpa had four wives altogether – some of them used to live together – so our family reunions were huge. Polygamy was not only expected, it was tradition and the secret to our survival. Back in the old country, way up in the mountains, mortality rates were very high among women and children due to childbirth complications and disease. If you don't produce a lot of sons, your legacy just dies off. Thus, to increase the chances of having children to help with farming, it was necessary to have as many wives as you could afford. Therefore, there was a huge influx of large Hmong families with their many kids that would be an impact to the local economy, the school system, the fish and wildlife industry, and the normal small town, conservative way of life in Willows.

My parents made me take 3rd grade again in the fall of 1988 because I was still so far behind. There were only a few Mexican families and two black families in the mostly white farming town. Then, suddenly, my people bombarded the town like a flash flood. Aside from a few people and organizations, nobody in the town knew who these "new Chinese" people were and how we ended up invading the town.

There was the Seventh Day Adventist Church, which helped sponsor a Hmong family and provided donated clothing, English language tutoring classes, and land for gardening.

There was Genevieve – an angel disguised as an elderly white lady English language tutor – who taught my parents and so many other Hmong folks how to read and write…for free. Thank you, RIP, Genevieve.

There was my one-time boss and closest family friend, Susan Rawlins, of the Willows Public Library. She was a saint disguised as a beautiful, strong, brave, and kind-hearted white lady with white hair and perpetual rosy cheeks. Of all the people who ever lived, this one singular person we owe the most to. She was the head librarian and advocate of peaceful Hmong integration, despite much contempt and retaliation from some of the town folk. Sue worked tirelessly to get many government grants to help educate and assist our people. She also hired me to mow her lawns and collect walnuts and pick cherries from her trees in the back yard for her. I had so many powerful conversations with her, especially during my trying teenage years. Sadly, most people will ever never know what kind of person she was and what she did for the town, for my people, and for my family. I've never met a more loving person in my life. She bravely fought for a long time with a perpetual smile, but was lost to cancer many years ago.

There was also Doe, Elizabeth, and the late Carol of the library. Carol's husband, Roy, was the one responsible for showing my brother and I how to play baseball and so many other amazing things about American culture.

Finally, there were a few officials from city hall and Social Services who knew about us as well but only because they had to deal with us. Few bothered to learn that we actually helped the CIA by siding with U.S. during the Vietnam War, how we sacrificed everything, how we were promised safety and military pay, how so many of our people perished during and after the war in the name of America, how we ended up in the refugee camps because the "real communists" were hunting us down for helping the U.S., and how we got here decades later after running for our lives the whole time. Most of the town folk never sought to understand who we were, choosing to give into fear, hate, and the easy way out…every time. The same was also true for most of our people – Hmong always preferring anonymity and freedom in their long nomadic history – who never made any real effort to accustom ourselves to the new land and its people. As time went on, most white people tolerated us as it was not "cool" to openly abuse or discriminate in public.

Over a decade later, as the kids grew up, most of the Hmong people moved out of the town, except for my parents and a few other families who were able find jobs and own businesses. The Hmong experiment "worked" depending on who you ask. If you asked my parents, they were able to seek a balance between the old world and new, and they were able to thrive here. If you asked a few white and Hmong people, they would say that they learned from the experience and were better for it. If you asked many white and Hmong people, it was as it was and it is what it is. If you ask the rest of the white and Hmong people, it was a relief that the experiment ended, so both could try to go back to their old way of life, however impossible it might be.

In the early days of the late eighties and early nineties, most of the Hmong experiences and interactions with white people were filled with fear, confusion, betrayal, mistrust, and outright hatred. I remembered being so scared of white people and their dogs. My cousins would run all over town picking low over-hanging fruits from the trees of our neighbors' houses, getting chased by dogs everywhere. My uncles would go on fishing and hunting sprees that locals feared would decimate the country side because they didn't know any of the laws regarding limits and seasons. Don't even mention the long, loud, and barbaric celebrations and ceremonies we would throw that would generate so much noise complaints. They didn't know what to do with us. Those early years were full of racist slurs from the white kids who no doubt learned it from their parents. Every day at school we were called gooks, commies, zips, ching-chongs, dog-eaters, and chinks, just to name a few that I could remember. There was no Google back then so for years I didn't know what any of those terms meant, but I knew it was a very bad thing. No day went by that I was not told to go back to my own country. They made sure we knew we weren't wanted here.

My cousins and I stayed close to each other at school to avoid being picked on and made fun of for our inability to communicate and for the clothes we wore which were scavenged free from kind church donations. I still cringe sometimes when I look through old pictures of that period where most of my clothes, especially the pants, were either always two short or two long.

The whole 3rd and 4th grade was nothing but a traumatic experience for me, as it was for my Hmong cousins and friends around my age. Looking back, that was probably why my Hmong peers had a much more negative view of the white people of Willows while the younger Hmong kids, who were several years younger, had a much more positive view. Most of them even had life-long best friends among their white classmates. They simply had more years of acclimation since pre-school or kindergarten, less of a language barrier to deal with, and less initial shock, thus less fear and discrimination later on. I see these Hmong kids nowadays and it fills my heart with joy and relief that they never had to go through what I had to go through in the camps and here in America during those early formative and tumultuous years. My hope is that it stays this way and no kid will ever have to know this side of human nature.

When I got to the fourth grade, because there were so many Hmong students at that time, the regular Murdock Elementary School couldn't house everyone so they put our class at the local Willows High School a couple of blocks away to the south. They separated some of the east wings just for the fourth graders. That's where I learned what a valedictorian was by talking to a high school teacher by chance. The teacher told me that the top student of the graduating class would be awarded the valedictorian award and most likely receive a full-ride academic scholarship to attend college. There it was! Sold! I was going to prove to everyone that I was not a stupid gook or a commie, that I belonged in this country, and I was going to make my parents proud as well as helping them with money for college! When I announced to everyone my intentions of becoming valedictorian, everyone laughed at me. The teachers were amused. My classmates all laughed at me, especially the white kids. My uncles and aunts patronized and mocked me for thinking I'm better than how I was born. My parents probably didn't believe it could happen but they went along with it. To my parents, education was the absolute top priority for them because they never had the opportunity to attend any formal schooling when they were young. My dad loved writing and calligraphy. My mom would always reminisce about the time she got punished when she was a curious young girl who disobeyed her mother and snuck out to the boys-only teachings when it was available in the village. While everyone laughed, I was the only one not laughing. I was dead serious. I didn't know how but it just felt right and I just had a confident feeling that I was going to find a way. I never remembered doubting myself. For me, there was no other outcome. I was going to do whatever it took to get it done, I just knew it. It was my ticket to Pepsi showers. I was all in. I was going to show everyone by being the valedictorian in nine years!

But how?

I was so far behind I couldn't even read first grade books like Dr. Seuss' Cat in the Hat, while everyone else was already reading these ridiculously hard 200-300 page books like The Indian in the Cupboard, The Secret Garden, and The Diary of Anne Frank. And my parents? My parents knew less than me. All I knew was that I was good at spelling because I could memorize well, so I proceeded to work hard at what I know and just memorized a page a day from every textbook in every subject. I would come straight home from school and take out my textbooks, read over and over each sentence quietly then out loud, then close the book and try to recall it, and kept doing it until I got it perfectly at least 3 times in a row. At the beginning, I relied entirely on memorization of every single word in sequence because most of the time I didn't know what the words meant. It seemed like an eternity, but soon I was able to piece whole sentences together, then paragraphs, and finally chapters. I did this for years. I didn't take much of a break because I couldn't afford to, mostly because my parents would always enroll my brother and I in summer school all the way till high school because they didn't want us to fall behind.

In about two and a half years, in the middle of the 6th grade, I finally got straight A's. The discipline and skills I've learned through my struggles gave me a strong foundation that would carry me through life. The most important lesson was that it doesn't matter how far behind you are in anything, with enough desire, commitment, and hard work, it's just a matter of time. More importantly, once I caught up to everyone else and surpassed them, I never looked back because I had developed the habits it took to achieve sustainable success. There was also another reward for getting straight A's, my father finally bought me tacos.

For years, I would have to watch my brother eat tacos at Taco Bell because only he got straight A's. We loved tacos more than any other food and that was my dad's incentive for us doing well in school.

I proceeded to keep getting straight A's from that point on all the way through high school and eventually became the valedictorian. I was not very well-liked in high school nor had many friends. It was probably because in grade school and middle school I was bullied and ridiculed so much that when combined with puberty, I was just always so angry and resentful. I had a good memory so I remembered every single word and act of unfairness, bullying, racism, mistreatment, and all the individuals who dealt them. For a young, impressionable, and impatient Hmong kid caught in a cultural identity war, seeing all the huge economic disparities, believing he has everything it takes to bridge that gap, and not fully comprehending emotions and fears yet, I had a really hard time in this town. That was also why I worked so hard to get the hell out of it as fast as I could. To this day, I still don't know which one was the better motivator, wanting to get out of Dodge as fast and as far as possible or earning a full-ride academic scholarship to help my parents out with money. If I had to bet my life on it, it would be the former.

I was all in on my goals of becoming valedictorian, top basketball player, and top tennis player in my school when I graduated, mostly to prove to everyone that they were wrong about us. To accomplish all three, while having been so far behind to begin with, meant I sacrificed popularity, child-hood, video games, TV, summer vacation trips, and goofing around. I wanted it so bad. I was so focused and worked so hard to make sure I achieved success. It was do or die for me, all in or nothing. Nobody was going to stand in my way. I saw everyone as a competitor. I held a grudge against anyone who said anything remotely bad about me, my cousins, or my people, and I just added it to the fire. I remembered them and plotted against them. I practiced, and worked extra hard to make sure I pay them back somehow someway – whether it was in PE class, the basketball gym, or in school. Nothing physical, I just wanted to destroy them with grades, sports, massive success, and then making sure they know it. I remember Susan Rawlins always telling me that the best revenge is great success. There was no other option other than great success. Most people, if they absolutely have to do something, they end up doing it. It's when there's choices and options that people end up not doing anything, half-assing everything, or failing at everything. Like my cousins always say, when there's a dog chasing you, I can guarantee that people will run much faster. There was no choice but to be all in. And because of that, I accomplished all I had set out to accomplish in high school.

Unfortunately, I never stopped to understand the principles that brought me my early success. I didn't learn from any of my successes in my early life. Back then, I was All In and didn't know any better. I just hated losing. Almost everything I did was with a do or die mentality. There was no other outcome, no plan B, no fear, and no other possibilities. There was no room in my mind and body for anything else but success. I knew what I wanted, I was passionate about it, I had laser-like precision focus, I didn't listen to the haters or the detractors, I was All In. I simply believed. I was just doing it because I wanted it so bad and somehow found a way to get it done by doing whatever it took, by being ALL IN.

It would take me over 17 years of being scared, struggling, and suffering before I realized why I was so successful in grade school and high school, but started failing afterwards in the real world. This book was written in part due to the epiphany I had after the whoopin' my father gave me. I wanted to give back to everyone who might be in the same position I was and hope this book serves as the whoopin' they need to stop their suffering and be all in on their dreams, passions, goals of being the best sales rep in the world or whatever, and live the life they are destined to live.

Chapter 2 #Truths

- Ignorance is no excuse.
- It doesn't matter how far behind you are, if you want it bad enough, you will find a way if you have the All-In Factor.
- When there's a dog chasing you, you run much faster.
- If you know what you want and you're All In, success is inevitable.

The Matrix/copyright 1999

Chapter 3: Belief is All That Matters

Neo: What are you trying to tell me? That I can dodge bullets?

Morpheus: No, Neo. I'm trying to tell you that when you're ready, you won't have to.

-The Matrix movie (1999)

That's right, most of you know this iconic scene from one of the most fantastic and influential movies of our time, The Matrix. After taking the red pill, Neo was awakened to the potential of being the savior of mankind, but he hadn't believed yet. During this scene, Neo was being shot at on top of a tall building by the agents and all he could do was try his absolute best to dodge the bullets. It was a valiant effort, but he still almost got killed. At the end of the movie, when he finally believed, he didn't even try to dodge the bullets; instead, he just stopped the bullets in mid-air, defeated the agents, and became The One.

Almost everyone believed in Neo, except for Neo, hence he couldn't stop the bullets. It did not matter that everyone believed in him, he didn't believe in himself therefore he couldn't become The One. When he didn't believe, all he could do was try to dodge the bullets as best he can without getting hit. This is the reality for most people. Everyone who knows you believe in you, except for you. Your friends, family, and co-workers have seen you excel at certain things and they know that you are quite capable of anything that you put your mind and energy into. The problem is you don't see it that way. See, nobody on this planet is completely stupid or incapable of success in any of the areas of their lives.

Most people, in fact, are all good at something, even experts at it, such as video games, computers, sports, cars, fitness, taking care of kids, taking care of pets…anything. What made you good or great at certain things in your life, you could use the same principles that made you good at it and apply it to the other parts of your life as well. However, most people tend to compartmentalize everything in their lives and believe that what makes them good in one area will not translate to another area of their life. They go through life never stopping to apply the lessons of their successes and victories to their ultimate dreams and goals. I know that while in the trenches, it is incredibly hard to look at the big picture, to step outside of yourself and look at yourself objectively from afar to see what others see. It's hard, but if people would only spend the necessary time to be with themselves, quietly, and really think about it, they will realize that because they are good at something, they have what it takes to be good at and ultimately be successful at anything else in life.

For example, my younger cousin, TC, is probably the most gifted athlete I've ever seen in my life, but he says he's just not good at talking, or career finding, or achieving goals, or getting his life together. He's said it a thousand times, "I'm just not good at anything but sports." This is because he believes that sports is the only thing he is good at in life. He believes that he is destined to suck at everything else. He says he's shy because he's just not good at being able to express himself or the right words to describe how he feels or what he wants. He says he's not good at speaking English so he just prefers to not say much so that people won't think he's dumb. He says he's just not good at work, reading, writing, planning, marriage, kids, or just about anything else other than sports. If only everything was as simple as sports, he would always say. "BS," I tell him, "Have you ever stopped to think for five minutes about what you are actually saying? Are there are no parallels you can draw from sports that would apply to the other areas of your life?" So, I had to slap him with the #truth.

The #truth is that all the basic principles and fundamentals of being good in sports applies to life as well, you just have to believe it. In fact, the principles of being good at anything could apply to any other area of your life. The truth is the truth, no matter who the messenger is. The truth is universal.

I told TC, "T, what made you good at sports was not a completely random thing that you were born with. You must BELIEVE that, Bro! Nobody is born good at anything. Some people are more naturally talented than others, but hard work is what developed those talents. You have to use S.L.G.P.P.D., Bro! And don't ask me why SLGPPD, I can't think of any clever acronyms so just go with it."

"You were good in sports because #1 above all else, you _started_. Starting is perhaps the hardest thing for most people to do. You can't ever do anything if you never start. Getting off the couch to go work out is the hardest part. Once you get to the gym, it's all actually very easy from there. But most people look and find excuses to not start. They're too tired. They didn't get enough sleep. They are embarrassed they may look bad. They are afraid they will fail. They don't think they'll be good enough. They don't believe that they have enough information, knowledge, or skills. They are too busy. They don't have time. It's going to be too expensive. It's going to take too long. It's too hot today. It's too cold. It's too dark. They're too broke. They'll do it tomorrow. Next week. Next month. Next year. The list goes on and on."

"So, #2, _liked_ it so you were All In! And when you like something, you tend to do more of it. Naturally, the more you do something, the better you get at it, and the better you get at something, the more you like it. This in turn reinforces your belief that you can do more of it, and the cycle repeats and you get better and better. It's really that simple! You don't like to lose in sports because you believe you are capable of so much more, because you've had great results in it, that's why you are ultra-competitive and rarely lose. You will do whatever it takes to win. Whatever it takes. All in. And when someone has this mentality about anything, they are normally good at it, if not great at it. It doesn't matter what it is. Most of your life you've won in sports because you've mostly gone up against people who don't want it as bad as you. They'll usually fold when the going gets tough and they start losing, unlike you. That is also why you will never beat me at golf! Because you've never learned how to beat me at golf because you've never done it! But I digress. Whatever happened, you believe that you will always win no matter how tough and how long it takes, so you never give up until you win. Money is never a factor in becoming good at any sport you pick up, somehow you always find the money to play it. The time you put in is enjoyed time and is never an issue either, somehow you always find the necessary time to be proficient at it, if not very good at the sport. All this just because you like it, imagine if you love it."

"It's the same thing for our cousins who love hunting and fishing. They are absolute geniuses at hunting and fishing. They know where all the best spots are at. They know what lures and ammo to use in every single situation. They spend so much money on gear that their trucks and tackle boxes look like mini Bass Pro Shop stores. They can't wake up early enough to do some chores, hang out with the family, or even keep a part-time job, but they can wake up at 3 A.M. to go hunting and fishing. That's why their wives complain about them all the time – even on Facebook for everyone to see! Me, I've never held a gun and I fish for everything with night-crawlers, just like what my dad taught me when I was 9 years old. The same goes for our other cousins who can't hold a job, but are the best video game players we've ever seen. They are always on the computer, PlayStation, X-box, or their phones. They know everything about these subjects and are always on top of the newest and greatest games, phones, or electronics, but can't keep a part-time job, and most them still live at home."

"Here's the kicker, or bonus, or whatever, if you really want to be good at something, be really successful at something, or achieve something really great, you have to learn to love it. You must be passionate about it, believe in it, be all in, and have a do or die mentality! If you really like something and believe in it, nobody has to pay you a dime to do it. You would even pay to do it. And when you do that, that's when you get really good or really great at it…maybe even greatest of all time at some point. You would invest time and money into it as well, just like your hobbies, your fun, and your play! See, the reason why companies have to pay you to work is because you don't really want to be there. You would rather trade in your time for the payment from a job that someone said you were worth. If it was for free, you would be outta' there so fast! But nobody has to pay you to play. You do well in that department all by yourself! You are all in that department. That's why you're so good at it!"

"Now don't get me wrong, there are some things in life that you just have to do that you just don't want to, but that doesn't mean you can't find ways to give it meaning that you could like or use as stepping stone for something else in life that you are passionate about. That may be your current job or position at work. If you have a part-time job and you hate it, that doesn't mean you won't be able to find something about the job that you could benefit from if you put forth some concentrated effort. You could use that position to propel yourself into a full-time position, then from there to a management position, then to a sales position, then into a business, and so on and so forth. You could find value in building your skills, developing your style, gaining experience, making life-long friends, and accumulating a strong network. There were so many countless days when I was an assistant manager – which was the toughest job in the company – for a Fortune 500 company called, let's just say…The Paint Company, when I just wanted to quit so bad. It's one of the most chew-you-up and spit-you-out places to work anywhere. There would be days where the customers were overly demanding, the boss was breathing down my neck, the phones were ringing off the hook, the facility was a mess, the employees didn't have their A-game, problems and issues left and right, I needed to send in some type of report before the end of the day, and nothing was going right at all, but I knew if I quit, I would have not learned how to solve situations like this in the future. So, I trucked on through and got it done. Every time I did it, I'm glad I did it. It wasn't fun, but I turned a problem into an opportunity to learn and I got something out of it. And that was what I liked about my job – the learning. That was the part I liked, that I found rewarding, that I believed in, and why I was all in on this job. The same thing goes for working out. Nobody likes the soreness. If you do it right, you will be sore. I promise you. That's the whole point. Most body builders or fitness people learn to like it. They see it as the building process. They see it as tearing something down to make it bigger. They see it as the necessary struggle that makes them stronger and better. They see it as a means to an end so they learn to enjoy it."

"And maybe, just maybe, if you are passionate about something enough, if you really, really believe in something enough, so much so that you'll even risk death for it, then that's when you'll be truly great – like Malcolm X, Martin Luther King, Jr, Gandhi, Nelson Mandela, Mother Teresa, Joan of Arc, Harriet Tubman, or any other great leader in history! Because the most powerful force on earth is the human soul on fire! Believe it! How do you think I went from nothing to the best sales rep in the construction industry? Instead of complaining like most, I just learned to like my worst fear, and went All In."

"So because you were all in, you #3 – _Googled_ it, if you didn't know something! Remember, ignorance is not an excuse. In this time and age, "I don't know" is just not an acceptable excuse. If you don't know about something, you would just simply Google it, just like what you did in sports. You watched videos about it and you read magazines about it. You watched Michael Jordan, Pete Sampras, and Tiger Woods on TV, you weren't afraid at all and spoke to everyone that was better than you about it, and most importantly, you thought about it all the time! You Googled it! You became a student. You focused on it. What you focus on is what will persist! It will grow! Out of sight, out of mind, right? If you are constantly thinking about it, that is what you will probably do more of, and the more you do, the better you get. The things that you don't bother to read up on, research about, and talk about…those things are normally things you don't care too much about. "I don't know" will not be an excuse anymore because you will research it. Like when I was the world's sorriest sales rep! One of the main reasons why I was so bad was because I had the "I don't know" mentality. It was a perfect excuse for me to keep being lazy and comfortable. Learning new stuff is uncomfortable, Man. New stuff equals change. And change is uncomfortable. Until the day I decided to change from the "I don't know" to All In."

"Most people would like to do this or do that, this goal, or this passion, or this dream…but then they realize that they are so far behind, so fear will creep in when they think about all the things that they don't yet know and all the research, time, and money it will take to figure it all out, then they'll quit. Don't do that. Be All In instead. You will find the answer for yourself if you truly want it!"

"And because you were all in, you #4 – _practiced_ it…consistently, every single day! After you Google it, you went and practiced it. Practice? We talkin' bout practice? Yes, Allen Iverson, we talkin' bout practice. You tried it. You tried it this way and that way. You found out for yourself, after countless hours, if it worked or it didn't or it did, but only after you made adjustments to your particular body type, skill set, or risk tolerance. But the point is that you put in massive action, massive time, and you put in the work, and you found out for yourself what truly works for you! You showed up even when you didn't feel like it. This may be the most crucial step to success in anything. The consistent showing-up step. Whether you didn't feel like it, whether you were sore, whether your wife or husband or parents or friends were mad at you, whether you were scared, tired, busy as hell, stressed, or something great was on TV, you showed the hell up! Every single day. Woody Allen famously said, "90% of success is just showing up!" It could be anything. If you show up every day with massive effort, you will be successful at it eventually. The level of your success will be directly proportionate to the level of your effort. Take fitness for example, if you want to be successful in losing weight and being fit, you gotta show up every day, whether you feel like it or not. You can hire all the trainers in the world, you can join all the gyms you want, you can read and research everything about fitness, but you gotta get yourself into the gym or on the road every single day or you'll never be fit. You can't afford to take days off or take shortcuts when you're 300 pounds, I promise you! You gotta show up, rain or shine, cold or hot, dark or light, sore or not, feel like it or not, busy or not, show up and put in some work! You don't even have to put in your best work or set personal records every single time you show up! You just gotta show up and put in some sweat equity! And you know you'll never regret it if you do. But what do most people do? They make a New Year's resolution to get fit, get all excited, then wait for a day when they feel like it before showing up and that generally means they never show up! Or they put in one really, really hard work-out, then get sore as hell and stop showing up! Or they'll manage to string together a couple of good days together, or a couple of weeks, or even a month, then they don't see any big fast results, so they quit showing up! Then they wonder why they failed massively every single year, year after year after year."

"Take being a successful sales rep. I was probably the worst sales rep in the history of the rep game when I first started. I wasn't the smartest, or the most talented, or the most natural at speaking. For goodness sake, I couldn't even look at people in the eye when I started because my grandpa had beaten that sense of "respect" into me so well growing up. My grandpa used to slap me upside the head every time I looked at an elder in the eye, telling me it was disrespectful. That was just part of our culture. After college, I worked as an assistant manager for The Paint Company and had to learn to overcome that problem. All the customers were older than me and I could never bring myself to look at them in the eye when dealing with them. The Koreans understood, the Hispanics didn't care, but many of the Caucasian customers thought I was disrespecting them. There were several complaints and I was written up once by my manager because one customer felt especially disrespected by me. I decided to make a pact with my full-time worker to help fight through this problem I had. We decided he was going to walk by and poke me in the ribs or in the back every time he saw me looking down when dealing with customers. He would poke me incessantly at least once or twice every 30 minutes when we first started. After months, the poking subsided to about once an hour. After about six months, it was about once or twice a day. After a year, it was only once or twice a week, and usually only because I was nervous with a large purchasing customer. After about two years, he never had to poke me again. I learned that I could overcome anything with diligent focused effort and my confidence skyrocketed. Most people would just run and hide when faced with such a built-in habit, but I decided to face my fears an overcome it. It took a huge amount of effort, consistency, discipline, and commitment. Because of this lesson, I quickly became store manager and then sales rep. I wasn't a good natural sales rep, but I knew I had all that it took to become one."

"Even though it was a long journey as a sales rep, I knew that if I just showed up every single day to my job with a determination of fighting through my fears of cold calling, getting rejected, looking stupid, and being disrespectful, then eventually I would succeed. I remember pulling up to customers' offices and just waiting in the car, conjuring up the courage to get out of my car to go knock on their doors. With some customers that weren't friendly or had an especially mean secretary, I would sometimes walk up to their door, almost knock with my knuckles almost touching the door, pull back, pretend I had an important phone call and take the fake phone call, walk back to my car to make some phone calls or answer some emails, make up an emergency to go take care of, and then just leave and waste all that time and effort. Sometimes I'd just sit there in the parking lot with the AC on until the customer shuts the office door and leaves to go home. Secretly, I was hoping they would hurry up and go run an errand or close up early. The one thing that kept me going was that I knew nobody else in the game had to go through what I had to go through. I knew most people, if faced with such obstacles would fold while I would triumph, so I persevered. Because of that, I brought my sales from $800,000 to over $2.4 Million annually in five years, with never a down year – 20% increase year over year."

"The only reason why I was successful was because I was there knocking on those doors even when I didn't want to and the customer either felt sorry for me or when they needed something, I was always there with a smile! I just showed up – every single week whether I felt like it or not! Put me against almost anyone for one really good day, where first impression is all that matters - immediate meet, greet, trust, where quick-close is a must, much like used-car sales, and I will lose 9 out of 10 times to any tall, good-looking young kid with no sales experience."

"I remember we had a regional sales blitz where all the reps were paired up to call on potential apartment complexes that didn't currently have commercial credit accounts with us. I was paired up with a young, up-and-coming rep to call on about 20 property management companies. The goal was to cold-call all these apartment complexes and persuade them to fill out commercial account credit applications so they can become purchasing accounts. We had a month to convert these prospects into accounts. We roshambo'd or rock-paper-scissored and I got the first 10 while my partner shadowed me quietly. After I was done, I had 1 out of 10 property managers interested in signing up. I just merely got their business cards and the names of their maintenance supervisors and promised them that I was going to follow up later. The kid effortlessly went and got 9 of his 10 prospects interested, if not, overly excited to sign up – especially the office ladies! However, at the end of the month, the final count for prospects that filled out and signed the application and became real commercial accounts were 9 for me and 1 for him. How did I do it? I showed up time and time again, followed up consistently, and built a relationship with the prospects. It was a lot of work, preparation, and persistence. Most of all, I was all in. The kid was naturally great at persuading, but if they didn't sign up immediately, he would have to actually work, prepare, and follow up. That was not his main strength. He didn't believe in that process as much as I did. He quit when they didn't call him back after a few tries. He got busy. It was too much work. He got frustrated. He wasn't used to that much work. Like most people, putting in a massive amount of work in one day when you're motivated is easy, but that leads to a massive amount of follow-up later, or what I call, the soreness – like after a really big workout when you haven't worked out in a long time. He wasn't used to showing up every day and putting in consistent work and follow-up. He was too sore from all the follow-ups. It was too overwhelming and he didn't want to experience that soreness again. I, on the other hand, have been showing up consistently, putting in incre-MENTAL work for years. I believe in it above all else. I believe that the secret to beating the odds in anything, especially if you're so far behind, is all *mental*, more specifically…incre-MENTAL. And that's how you're going to be good or great at anything. By believing in yourself, by being all in, and incre-MENTALLY showing up every day and putting in the necessary work it takes to get better inch by inch, bit by bit, until you look up one day and there's nobody up anymore, they are at the same level as you or below you."

"See, TC, many sales reps are way better than me on when it comes down to just one day or one sale, but I'll beat them at least 9 out of 10 times when it comes to real sales, where it's not a one-off deal and relationships have to be earned over time! In fact, I don't know too many sales positions anymore like on TV, the movies, or as previously perceived where it's all about a quick impressive two-minute elevator pitch and immediate close. How did I become a top sales rep? Because I learned through experience and I believe deeply in some of these fundamentals through trial-and-error, and probably mostly through pure necessity. That is why I will show up every, single, day to fight through my fears for what I truly want! This almost guarantees success in anything you do. I mean, if you want to be a good husband or wife - show up, practice, every single day, consistently, even when you don't feel like it! If you want to be a good parent - show up, practice, every single day, even if you're busy! If you want to be a good businessman - show up, practice, every single day, even if you've lost a ton of money! If you want to be a good athlete - show up, practice, consistently, every single day, even if you're not the most talented! If you want to lose weight and be fit - show up, practice, consistently, every single day, even if you're sore! If you want to be a good sales rep…you get the idea! If you want to be good at anything in life, you just have to show up, practice consistently, every single day, with some enthusiasm for bonus points, even when you don't feel like it! And if you want to be great, you will have to believe."

"Because you were all in, you #5 – _played_ it until you got the results you were looking for. After you Googled it, you practiced it, then put it into play and measured the results to see if you are up to par with the course, your competition, and your goals and results. You gave it enough time and patience to see it through. If the results were adequate, you kept it up. If it wasn't, you went back to Google some more, tweaked it accordingly, practiced it and played it. You repeat this until you get satisfactory results!"

"And lastly, #6, you *didn't quit* until you achieved that level of success you sought, that which you envisioned. You persisted. You persevered. You did whatever it took. You were sure you already accomplished it, all the way to when you actually accomplished it. You kept at it until you beat that person in front of you and the next until you beat the competitor you wanted to beat, including yourself. You were all in! When you're all in, it was just a matter of time."

Just to bring the point home, I told him, "Look, TC, I'm not the only one who's ever said this." I told him about a conversation my brother and I had about him back at the end of 2013.

My brother said, "Jeez, I wish we were as good at things naturally as our cousin, TC. That guy made it look so good and without any effort, we had to call him, Silk. He was smooth as silk, no effort whatsoever. He picked up things quickly and became the best out of all of us at almost anything. Basketball – he picked up the ball and in two seconds, had the smoothest, quickest, most consistent mid-range jumper out of all of us. Tennis – he picked up a tennis racquet for the first time and in half a season, became the second-best player on the team next to you, BOLO, and you had played for 4 years already. Not only that, when he decided to marry his Hmong wife, while his entire family was against it, that guy had the audacity to disown his entire family in order to marry that girl. And he got two freakin' degrees in college in the process too! Without any help from anyone! What the hell? Guaranteed, we wouldn't be able to do that! That dude did whatever it took. That dude was all in! That's why he succeeded! But look at him now, whatever happened to him? He's about to blow his entire life up!"

I reminded TC about when he was going through the toughest point of his entire life at the end of 2013. His marriage was a complete disaster. He had two little girls, but they weren't enough. He was going nowhere fast at his department assistant manager job at the local Wal-Mart in Chico, California. His immediate family was no better – with his father now separated from his mother and they were manipulating the kids against each other. His in-laws weren't in much better shape. The two families still resent each other. He had no friends left. All the friends and relatives that he admired had moved out and on with their lives. He said to me this was the loneliest time of his entire life.

When he finally did call me, it was because most of the fear had left him. He realized that once you're at the absolute rock bottom, fear just doesn't have the same effect anymore because it can't hurt you anymore than it already has. He said he was tired of being tired. He said he was sick of being sick. He said that if he didn't get out of Northern California soon, he will probably die. He was ready to give up his family and his entire life to start over if it comes down to that. I found him a nice job at my old company right before I left to start my failed business and he dropped everything within a week to come down. He lived on my couch for six months, worked out with me early every morning at 4 A.M., and slowly started to climb out of his hole.

As time passed so did the pain. He grew stronger physically and incre-MENTALLY, and started to believe that he could be more than just good at sports. He looked back and realized that he could have anything he wanted and be successful at anything he wanted if he only believed in it above all else, like when he wanted to marry his wife, his girl, The One, despite the backlash from his whole family. He wanted it bad enough. He was All in on her. Do or die, ride or die. If he wasn't, he most certainly would have taken the easy way out. He would have found an excuse when things got real, when things got tough, when things didn't go as planned, when he was scared, when he was in doubt, when he wasn't feeling it, and when it hurt. He started to believe that – just like sports – he could be successful at anything else in life as well if he was All In. At the writing of this book, I would like to report that TC's marriage is disgustingly envious, he spends more time than ever with his kids, he has already excelled exponentially at work, especially at sales, has even opened a tiny side business in which he plans to grow into the business of his dreams, and has traveled and seen more than he ever thought was possible. All In.

Chapter 3 #Truths

- The only belief that matters is self-belief.
- How to get good at anything: S.L.G.P.P.D.
  - #1. Start it.
  - #2. Love it.
  - #3. Google it.
  - #4. Practice it.
  - #5. Play it.
  - #6. Don't Quit it.
- Show up every day.
- It's all incre-MENTAL.
- Everyone is good at something.
- Everyone can be good at anything else.
- Remember: S.L.G.P.P.D.

Chapter 4: #Truth

Towards the end of high school, when my goals were seemingly inevitable, the very same kids who told me that I was a stupid gook and told me to go back to my own country, began saying that it was because I was lucky and smart, that's why I was going to be valedictorian. Lucky to have been so poor and so behind in school? Right. Smart? It couldn't have been the countless days and nights studying memorizing words and not having much of a childhood here in America.

That was one of my most important lessons in life. See, that's what unsuccessful people like to attribute the success of other people to – luck, money, talent, genius, knowledge, or any number of things to take away from the real truth – so that they could lie to themselves and sleep at night. The #truth was that it takes countless hours of hard work, countless hours of suffering, and countless hours of massive determination, focus, and stress.

What they don't realize is that the lies they tell themselves is what is holding them back. What they don't realize is that luck has very little to do with success. Yeah, so some people do get lucky and hit the lottery, but that's very little. Most of them actually work very hard at trying to win the lottery. They spend a lot of time and money going to the liquor store or gas stations and buying those tickets. If most of them put as much time and energy into actually trying to excel at their job, starting a business, creating something, building something, or investing in something, they would probably already be rich. That has a much higher chance at getting rich than winning the lottery. Even my uncles and aunts who have worked on the farm for my parents and have seen my parents struggle all those years to make money and still struggling, they say that it was because my parents were lucky, that's why they are successful. Everything was just given to them by some higher deity. God must love them or they must have done something wonderful in their past life. Are you kidding me?

I used to get so angry and say, "Really!?! We all came to America at the same time. You guys chose to live on welfare, buy new cars, hunt and fish every day, never had a real job since you came here. To this day, you can barely speak a lick of English after being here in America for over two decades, and my parents are lucky? That's your explanation? My parents got off welfare in two years. They volunteered. That means working for free! They worked every type of job imaginable and saved everything. I mean everything! For goodness sakes, while you guys were buying new cars, my parents bought me 3 tacos for 99 cents at Taco Bell for getting straight A's! That's how they rolled! They went to night school and got their high school diplomas! They learned English. They were the first to start working. They grinded, saved, hoped, and learned incre-MENTALLY. They struggled at the bottom of the middle class for a decade which is actually worse financially than being on welfare! They were the first to take a risk and buy a house when all of you were against it. You even convinced my grandparents to criticize them, and also convinced me to be a little embarrassed of my parents for being such fools – thank God they didn't listen to anyone. Your math was short sighted but it worked on me as I was only 13 years old at the time. I mean, rent is only $400 a month and you keep your savings, why pay $700 per month after putting all your life savings into buying the house? You won't pay it off until 30 years later. You're better off living the dream for 30 years after struggling in the Refugee Camps in Thailand for so long, come on, relax, don't be stupid, that's too risky! Right? Wrong! Then they were the first to start their own business, by buying a farm! I remember my first summer of manual labor digging those strawberry trenches by hand with my cousins, getting paid with Gatorades! That was what made me never want to be a farmer ever! Then you guys saw my parents work every single day from 3 A.M. to 10

P.M., 7 days a week, 365 days a year, no vacations! My parents would pay you guys to help pick strawberries and produce. Most of you quit by noon! You couldn't handle the heat! Some of you had heat stroke! Shoot after her skin cancer surgery for being out in the sun year after year, my mom was out there the very next day in the sun with a big ole hat, a ton of lotion, and lots of pain-killers! You were their brothers and sisters! You saw them from the very beginning struggling! You barely lent a single hand and just mocked them the whole time! And now you say they were lucky so that's why they are successful?!"

There's no such thing as luck in being successful and staying successful. That's why the successful stay successful year after year in the face of a bad economy or whatever external factors that may have occurred. It's just who they are. That's also why most lottery winners go broke again within a year. They are not successful in their minds, in their habits, and in who they are as people. They just got real lucky. After a year of doing what poor people do best - spend on things with no ROI and not saving - they go broke again, and most are in more debt than they've ever been.

You are poor because of who you are, what you focus on, what your habits are, what your parents taught you, what your reality and perspectives are, what you believe in, and what actions you take. If you don't believe this, go read about the recent ground-breaking study conducted by researchers at Johns Hopkins University and detailed in the book, *The Long Shadow: Family Background, Disadvantaged Urban Youth, and the Transition to Adulthood* (Russell Sage Foundation, 2014). They studied 790 Baltimore schoolchildren from various backgrounds and neighborhoods for over 25 years from when they were kids to how they turned out as adults. In the book, Karl Alexander, the sociology professor in charge of the study, makes the point that a family's resources and the doors they open cast a long shadow over children's life trajectories to conclude that the poor stayed poor and the rich stayed rich. But it did also state that education and hard work could lift people from the inner city out of poverty – however exceptional those cases may be. I've seen this exception in my parents. It takes all the things I will explain in this book. It takes belief, owning the #truth, doing what is required, and never giving up despite the incredible odds stacked against you. It took over two decades of building and becoming successful before they could realize the success they sought. All the cases that I've ever read, seen, heard, or been a part of, there was no "luck" involved when it comes to lifting one's self and one's family from the inner city, from the jungles, or from poverty. It always takes a massive amount of help from other people, education, investment, belief, responsibility, risk, hard work, sacrifice, and perseverance.

Also, there's no such thing as over-night success. What most people don't see is that the so-called "over-night success" took many years of toiling in the trenches, struggling countless days and nights, and getting better every day, waiting for the opportunity to come by so they could take advantage of it and shine. That was when people saw them. They prepared in the dark. They worked hard in the dark. They cried but didn't give up in the dark. They were getting ready for when the opportunity came, and when it did, they latched on to it and rode it into the limelight. It took years. What most people don't get is that you have to be ready for the opportunity, because if you're not ready, you're just waiting and waiting but never preparing, when it does come, you'll miss it like you always do. It would be too fast for you to grab on to it or even see it at all.

This was the case when I bought my dinky little 2-bed, 2-bath townhome at the end of 2007, in Lake Forest, CA at the height of the housing bubble before the crash. I paid close to half a million for it! I always said someday I'll own a bunch of real estate, but I never sat down to ever pick up a book about it, ask questions, or research about it. I just wanted a house and when everyone was buying, I did what the pack did and bought too. I let my wife make all the decisions and just signed away because I thought I could afford the ARM loan until the value goes up like every said it would then I could flip it and make a boat-load of money like everyone said I would.

Then when the economy crashed, my wife lost her job, the property dropped more than 60% in value, and we lost it a couple of years later. I promised myself that I will never *not* be ready again. It was all mental…incre-MENTAL. I made a decision. I will always be prepared, learn for myself the things that are important to me, and be ready for what I want when it shows up.

Success is when preparation meets opportunity, said Zig Ziglar, the Michael Jordan of Sales. You always have to be preparing for your next step, job, or opportunity. A sales manager buddy once told me his secret to climbing the corporate ladder so fast and so young. He said, I'm never doing my current job, I'm always just training for my next job. Where ever you are in life, you have to find and take advantage of things that you can learn and build upon for the next part of your job, career, business, or life. If you don't or you're too afraid to be all in, you'll be like most people, just waiting, hating, not wanting to work harder, complaining, crying, suffering, not getting anywhere in life, and blaming everyone and everything for your "lack" of opportunity and the endless reasons why you "can't" do your job or why you "can't" be successful. Here's the kicker, it takes as much work to suck as it is to be successful.

It's not because you're a nice guy why you finish last either, like the old saying goes. You falsely think that the reason you aren't successful is because you're a nice guy, thus you falsely come to the conclusion that everyone who is successful must be an asshole. They will cheat, lie, steal, and kill whoever is in their way to get whatever material things they desire, that must be why they are successful. But not you, you're a nice guy or gal, you would rather just be nice than an asshole. Let the assholes be successful for they will rot in hell. That's what I used to tell myself. Boy was I wrong.

As I got older, started to network, and talked to many successful businessmen, I realized that it's not purely because assholes win and nice guys finish last. It's because assholes normally don't take no for an answer, they don't settle, they don't care about your meaningless feelings, they know exactly what they want, and they will do whatever it takes to get the job done, no matter who is in their way. Nice guys do win too, but only those who don't settle, know what they want, and will do whatever it takes to get it. You don't have to be an asshole to do that. Where there's a will, there's a way. You don't have to cheat, lie, steal, and kill to get what you want. You can be strong and firm and focused without being an asshole. You can be a nice guy and succeed. In fact, the most successful people I've ever met are probably the kindest and most generous people – willing to spend the time talk to me, t0 answer my questions, and to help me. Most "nice" guys are just weak – weak discipline, weak beliefs, weak ideas of what they want, and weak habits and actions – that's why they don't demand what they want, they don't fight for it hard enough, they try to protect and hold on to what little they have for dear life, and they usually lose to "bad" guys who "don't care about anyone's feelings" who just "take" what they want.

It's not a secret either or a shortcut. Beware those things that promise you there's a secret to getting rich or fit quick, working only an hour a day, or working from some beach somewhere starting from scratch. The #truth is that success is about showing up every day with a plan and a purpose, putting in a massive amount of sweat equity, and not quitting until you succeed. There may be a few people out there that are massively successful and currently only working a few hours a week from some exotic location, but I guarantee you it wasn't because of some magical shortcut or secret that they woke up one day from being poor and then suddenly became rich. If anything, it took them years of hard work, soul-searching, and trial and error to create this lifestyle they now enjoy. In life, there is no magic pill. You can't buy abs.

The #truth was, "You're over thirty years old, you're a grown ass man, what were you thinking? Doing back-flips? Trying to impress people? Trying to tell people off? Fracturing your leg in two places, getting mad at me for not having any sympathy for you when I took you to the hospital? Then joking about it to your friends on Facebook, saying stuff like #awesome, #epic, and #boom! Well, here's the #truth...#brokenleg #stupid #immature #youvegotafamily #Iwilldivorceyouifyoudoanotherbackflipagain!" My wife posted that on my Facebook page, all my friends laughed a good ole time, I was so mad at her that I deactivated my account and didn't join back for a couple of years until after I had recovered from my failed business, almost failed marriage, almost failed parenthood, and almost failed life. Now I own the #truth. I'm a grown ass man. No more back-flips. No more BS. No more Lala Land. I had to own up to the #truth before I was able to work on the things that truly mattered to me. Like Jerry Maras said, if you're not focused on the right things, then you're focused on the wrong things, and if you're always in the shit, you're always concerned about other people's games, and not focused on your own game, you'll never be a great golfer. Golf has many parallels to life and this is especially true.

Another #truth I learned was that Pepsi showers are highly overrated. After the last day of college, I went to the local Ralphs supermarket and bought me a 24-pack of Pepsi to take showers in as a reward for completing college, finding a great job, and celebrating a part of my dream coming true. I went into the dorm shower, opened every single can and sat them all down on the hard tile. Then I proceeded to pour every single can all over myself. While it tasted wonderful, let me tell you, it burned my eyes and face! I also learned it was a mess to wash Pepsi out of hair! These days, I'm still All In on my Pepsi shower dream, but as a figurative one instead of literal, for obvious reasons.

Chapter 4 #Truths

- The number one thing that holds people back is themselves.
- There's no such thing as luck if success is who you are.
- There's no such thing as an over-night success.
- Nice guys can finish first.
- Success is not a secret.
- If you're not focused on the right things, you're focused on the wrong things.
- #Truth: Pepsi showers are highly overrated.

Chapter 5: I Am

Perhaps the two most important words in any language that I learned in my short time on earth is this: I am. I have learned that everything that comes after these two words will determine your belief and therefore your destiny. It's what you believe. It is your own self-talk, self-doubt, and self-concept. Most of the time, it occurs without you not even being aware of it. Most of the time, it's automatic, it's unconscious, and that's when it's the most dangerous. Some people will go through life sadly not ever being aware of this simple yet most powerful device. The really sad part is that they were the ones who were in complete control the whole time. They believed that they were never in control of who they are, their thoughts, emotions, actions and what they have in life, when in fact, at any point in time, they could have simply chosen differently. What you constantly tell yourself and others is a result of the unconscious beliefs you have about yourself. Further, what you have in your life right now – your body, your finances, your success, your current job, the people you surround yourself with – then is a physical manifestation of those unconscious beliefs. This was all that separated my parents from my uncles and aunts. This was all that separated me from my cousins and the majority of my people. It was not anything else tangible. It was just the All-In Factor. It was all mindset. It was all incre-MENTAL.

When TC said "I am good at sports, but I'm just not good at anything else in life," it literally became his reality, a self-fulfilling prophecy. As long as he continues saying those words, his reality will stay the same. As long as he says, "I am…good at sports," he will always be good at sports, no matter what sport. He will be able to pick it up quick, excel at it, and be competitive at it. As long as he says, "I am…not good at reading," he will never pick up a book and that is why it took me years to force him to read <u>The Alchemist</u> and <u>The 7 Habits of Highly Effective People.</u> As long as he says, "I am...not good at speaking English," then he will never be good, even though we both came to America at the same time 28 years ago. Somebody made fun of his English a long time ago in grade school and he believed he wasn't good at it, so to this day he fears communicating his feelings and thoughts, and he hates public speaking of any sort. As long as he says, "I won't" and "I can't" and "I'm just not..." then just stick a fork in him, he will NEVER do it.

Most people have one bad experience and for the rest of their lives they have it in their heads that anything remotely similar is going to be an automatic fail which normally ends up being true for them. This in turn reinforces more failed experiences in the future. The same goes for people who say, "I'm not going to like <u>insert subject</u>," without even trying it once. I said that same exact sentence to my wife a long time ago about golf when she bought me some golf lessons for Christmas. As it turns out, I love it more than I've ever loved any sport.

When you say you *can* then you can actually put S.L.G.P.P.D. into action. You keep focusing on it, actually produce a plan, and work at it for as long as it takes, then you are pretty much guaranteed success. That means you believe in your heart and in your mind that you will do whatever it takes to get it done, it's just a matter of time. Muhammad Ali said he was the greatest of all time before he was even a champion.

On a much much smaller scale, I had to start calling myself "El Presidente" way before I ever received the coveted President's Club award for highest sales achievement as a rep at my old company. I started wearing a tie when everyone else was wearing polos and jeans. I bought and started using expensive, heavy, chromed-out $100 Cross pens because it gave that extra nudge of confidence, while everyone else had cheap 99-cent company-logoed pens. I started carrying around $200 real leather-bound padfolios because it made me feel more "executive" and "VIP", while everyone else was using Post-it notes or scratch pads to take orders. Everyone started calling me "VIP" as a joke at first because I was a nobody who they thought was only pretending and will never become anything special. They all laughed at me, except for me. I believed that I was VIP – even though my results were quite the opposite – until I was…and in the end, that's all that matters.

That's what the real pros do. I've seen it time and time again. To the untrained eye, the weak, the unsuccessful, the unbeliever, the poor, these pros can seem like real arrogant a-holes. These unbelievers reason it this way because they themselves have never failed enough times or tried enough times to know what they can and can't do. To those who have accomplished success, especially at a high level, they know that nothing is impossible as long as the passion, the will, and the belief is there. Shooter's roll, member bounce, Midas touch, call it whatever you like, the better they are, the more it seems, they just keep finding ways to win against any odds.

To this day, I have had to translate English into Hmong in my head, then Hmong into English, then speak it back to people. That is something I still struggle with and may never get over it. I'm always at a disadvantage when going up against natural born English speaking reps. It was also a false belief I told myself for years why I will never be good enough and why I will never be a great rep. I've always believed that I was just not meant to be a sales rep as everything was just set up against me from my people, to my grandpa, to my upbringing, to my resources, to my skills, and to my destiny. I got beat up. To be more accurate, I beat myself up. Nobody did it. It was all incre-MENTAL. I did it to me, bit by bit, day by day, year by year. When I got good, when I was All In, it was also incre-MENTAL as well. It was only until I made the decision to stop my suffering – enough was enough – that I slowly started to crawl out of the abyss of mediocrity. How did I do it? Incre-MENTALLY.

It all started with wanting to be as great as I knew, deep in the back of my mind, that I could be, instead of living in Suckville. But the fears, the doubts, the self-mutilating talk, the lies, and the disbelief I had was so incredibly hard to overcome. It was ingrained in me. It was seared into the back of my head. Every positive thought of ever being successful was always quickly, deceivingly, and masterfully overridden by the deep-rooted, unconscious, and subversive conditioning that was implanted decades ago into the very fabric of my being. In the history of mankind, there was, is, and will always be only one thing that will defeat the horrors and atrocities of the human condition and that is the human soul burning at a hotter inferno than the heart can contain. You have to be all-in to know what I'm talking about. And when you do, you will know that it was all inside you the whole time.

Think back to your own beliefs, your own self-talk, and your own experiences. What you think, what you say, what you focus on, what your experiences have been, and what you believe will become your reality. Until that belief changes, your reality will persist and you will not be able to change it. The human mind is so advanced, so intricate, and so powerful that unless your will is strong, trained, and filled with enough purpose, it will run you and take over your life for as long as you let it. Unfortunately for you, your mind and your fears work so well together that it will take more than everything you've got right now and more to overcome it, and take control of your life. The mind is like an onion, with so many unfathomable layers to it. You may be able to peel one layer away and another, but before you know it, another layer has just appeared. You'll be digging through that labyrinth for a while, but from left field, the previous layers have already popped back up and you'll be back at square one. It is almost impossible for external forces to peel those layers off. The only thing strong enough to defeat fear is belief. Every decision is a see-saw between fear and belief. Your belief and what you want must be greater than your fears and your doubts. If you constantly give into fear, blame, the past, excuses, and doubts, then you need to keep defining your wants and beliefs until it is so clear and so strong that you stop giving in to fear. Good luck, but you can do it. For example, for years, every single time my wife and I would get into arguments over the littlest stuff, she and I would go right back into the past and start throwing out blame, names, and all the things we said, did, or didn't do to each other. When that happens, it was always does because we wanted to blame the other person and make the other person the bad guy more than what was really important, which was our marriage, our love, and our future. The proof is in the pudding, in the decisions and choices you make. If what you say you want is really important, then you would choose that every time instead of other things that don't even matter. Pure and simple.

It is absolutely critical that you believe because a strong belief determines how far, how high, and how long you can go. If you believe your limit is massive or limitless, then you will put forth the necessary massive action and effort required to match that limit. Just like in sales or anything else in life – it's basically a numbers game – the higher the action and effort level, naturally the more the results. That is why high achievers always seem to find a way to achieve more in life no matter the odds stacked against them, hence the terms winners win and the rich get richer. They usually just put in more effort because through experience, they know they've done it before and can do it again and again. They don't let problems, set-backs, no's, objections, or obstacles get in their way. They keep at it until they find a way to succeed. Conversely, the opposite is true. That's why sometimes when you get in a rut, it just seems like there's no way to climb out of it. Losers lose and the poor get poorer. Hmong people are born to tragedy. Tragedy and suffering is our destiny, as my aunts would always tell me. I've been there and I've seen most of my people get stuck in this rut. It's all we've ever known, it's what we believe, and it's what we are as a majority. It takes a very few special people to break out of the jungle or the hood here in America. Think about it, if all you see is poverty, all you know is poverty, and all you believe that is available to you is poverty, it is almost impossible to climb out of that rut to experience success and believe that you can be successful. But that's why belief is so important.

The ability to believe is the one thing that separates us human beings from the regular animal. Yes, physically, it's the bigger evolved brain that started it all, but the concept of belief is what really separates us from the rest of the animal kingdom. You could call it creativity. I call it belief. We are the only animals capable of making up stuff like imaginary countries, borders, rules, religion, laws, money, baseball, football, basketball, soccer, and numerous other made up stuff. We can convince ourselves that other human beings will play nice, until they don't, then they end up in jail or dead, such as criminals who don't abide by the rules and the laws. Take a lion, a tiger, or a bear and tell them that they have to abide by our made up laws, live as normal citizens, and try to trade our made up credit cards for their food and they'll rip your face off.

We believe in religion so that we can live a more fulfilled life here on earth and hope to live in a better place after we pass. That is why people who are willing to die for their beliefs are so powerful. That's because those who don't play by our made-up rules are the ones who are in control. Reality is what we believe it to be, aside from some basic laws of physics. The rest of us think we are all safe, then boom, a bomber who believes in his cause enough to blow himself up comes along – who doesn't play by the same rules – and wreaks havoc on families and the whole entire belief system. We can pack thousands into any airport, tens of thousands at a concert, over 100,000 people into NFL stadiums for the Superbowl, or millions at New Year's Eve in Times Square every year, and believe that we are safe because everyone believes the same thing. All it takes is one screwed up person who believes in his cause enough to die for it and everything changes for those involved.

Conversely, the other side is true too. You don't have to be screwed up. As shown by the lense of history, most of society could be the ones all screwed up believing that slavery is okay, until others who believed in the opposite rose up to abolish slavery. The same goes for the Nazis who believed in the superiority of the pure Aryan race, until the world united to stop them. Belief is what our planet's entire civilizations were built upon. Our beliefs in ourselves, each other, our causes, and in our society is what shaped history – from victories to wars to discoveries to landing on the moon. Belief comes first. If we didn't believe that the earth was round and that we could sail across the oceans, we wouldn't. If we didn't believe we could land on the moon, we wouldn't.

Seeing other people succeed makes us believe that we may be able to succeed as well. If I never saw my friends doing P90X and dropping over 100 pounds, I wouldn't believe it could be done and I would never be as fit as I am now. If I didn't learn from other people that you could wake up at 3:30 A.M. every weekday to go work out, I wouldn't have tried it and I wouldn't believe it could be done. Moreover, if I didn't read in a magazine article that you could average only 4-5 hours of sleep a night and still be fine, I wouldn't have tried it and I wouldn't believe it could be done. By the way, if you do the research yourself like I did and try this, don't tell your bosses or co-workers about your daily 20 minute naps at 12:30 P.M. or they'll think you're just lazy and try to sabotage you.

Because I saw other people become motivational speakers, writers, artists, eating the best foods, playing great golf, owning businesses, owning real estate, traveling the world, and spending quality time with the people they love, I believed that it was possible for me as well. Because of belief, I now enjoy creating and living all those passions. None of this would be possible without belief. My hope is that by being true to myself, fulfilling my dreams, and living my passions, I too will be a possibility for other people as well. If I can be that belief just for one person, then all of this would be worth it. Long story short, stop saying you can't, start saying you can, and stop saying I'm not, start saying I am.

Chapter 5 #Truths

- Your own self-talk is supremely important
- Every decision is a battle between belief and fear
- Winners have high beliefs about themselves
- Losers have low beliefs about themselves
- Belief equals possibilities

Chapter 6: Crazy

Steve Jobs said, "The ones who are crazy enough to think that they can change the world are the ones who do." Now that I've suffered for so long and got out from the depths of hell, I've realized that crazy is actually not a bad thing to be called. It means you're doing something right.

There's clinical crazy, then there's the perception of crazy. The clinical definition of crazy is defined as someone mentally deranged, especially as manifested in a wild or aggressive way. Then there's the perception of crazy, which is what people call you if you become overly enthusiastic or obsessive about someone or something, you're too extreme, you're not normal, or you're not average.

When I was skinny-fat and 165 pounds, it was normal. Gaining the Rep-15 in three months when you become a rep was normal. Fast foods, coffee, and energy drinks make up the normal rep diet. Nobody had any sympathy for me. It was okay. When I would complain, people would just say, "Shut up, you're freakin' skinny!" I was 5'3" and 115 pounds dripping wet going into college. I had a hard time gaining weight, always skinny. After college, I was 5'5" and a ½" with shoes, and 125 pounds – still skinny and in shape. Then wife, life, and work happened. Ten years later, a whole decade went by faster than the blink of an eye, and I'm at 5'5-1/2" and 165 pounds. That extra 40 pounds at my height was a lot to carry around all day, every day. I was wearing large dress shirts for work because smalls and mediums wouldn't fit my gut, even though I was a natural small. The waist would roll over resembling a wrinkly upside down pear around my sad drooping torso. If I didn't tuck the shirts in, they would look like I was in a dress almost touching my knees. The sleeves would get bunched up and hang out over my knuckles so I'd always roll up my sleeves. My wife would take pot-shots at me and say stuff like, "Hey, that belly makes a nice food tray," or "Nice one pack," or "You're old and fat, you should probably pick up an old man's game like golf!" In fact, she bought me golf lessons for Christmas one time and I threw it away, electing to get mad at her, drink beers, sit on the couch, eat junk food, and watch all my favorite TV shows. I was always tired and could barely get it up, nor could I see it when looking down unless I moved my gut out the way first. The point was it seemed normal. All my friends were getting old and fat, even though I was just 30. In fact, they were all fatter and in worse shape than me. My brother was even worse. All my cousins were even worse than my brother. I was still considered skinny compared to all my co-workers and everyone I knew. It was normal so who cares. Nobody had sympathy for me. What I saw, what was around me, and what the general narrative was in America confirmed it – I was normal. All things considered, I was actually better than normal. The problem was I knew in the back of my mind and at the bottom of my heart that something was wrong with this "normal". If it was right, my back wouldn't be hurting and giving out all the time. If it was right, I would have more energy. If it was right, I would be able to look at myself in the mirror and not cringe. If it was right, I'd have the drive to make love to my wife. Back then, she actually wanted me, in fact, she begged me. Instead, I trained her to not want it anymore for a long time. If it was right, I'd be happy with normal. Unfortunately, I was miserable.

I remember my wife used to tell me, "I hate doing things with you because you can't do anything normal! It's always all or nothing with you! You're too competitive! It's no fun for anyone else! You're just so intense, nobody likes you!" She would get mad at me, blame me, cry, be embarrassed of me, and try to change me. She succeeded. I was four years into my marriage, six years into my career as a corporate man, and neither going according to what I had imagined at this point in my life. I started thinking that something was wrong with me. In an attempt to get my wife to like me and my company to start noticing me, I started practicing the art of self-deprecation, being a jokester, and being a goofball. That's when everything else really fell apart. In trying to please everyone, I pleased no one, including myself. I didn't even know who I was anymore. Most of my friends had graduated and moved out and away to work and live, or we simply just lost touch. I didn't even know what I wanted in my life anymore.

I was doing what my wife wanted but she still wanted to divorce me. I was doing what all my other peers were doing – even though it was awkward at first, I got good at it – but I was still getting passed up for promotion after promotion. After getting passed up time after time, interview after interview, and hopes crushed time and time again, most people often do two things: they start becoming bitter, resentful, give up and display it openly or they start becoming bitter, resentful, give up and hide it. The former will tell everyone about it including the bosses, co-workers, competitors, and even customers. They become a morale killer and a liability. From there, it's only a matter of time before management is forced to take action due to a variety of incidents, big and small. The latter, will normally only tell those they're closest to and those willing to listen. The incidents will probably take longer to occur and is not as noticeable if even noticed. Both will start declining in performance and morale – some more gradual than others. Both will start asking around and looking for other jobs, exploring their options, but normally no opportunities will be found soon, if ever. Some will leave, some will stay. Those who stay will probably turn into what I call The Typical Jose.

Chapter 6 #Truths

- There's a difference between clinical and perception of crazy
- Be crazy
- Being average is worse than crazy
- Trying to please everyone, you please no one

Chapter 7: The Typical Jose

The Typical Jose is an employee who has been there at the store, office, facility, or territory longer than anyone else. He knows everyone in the business and everything about the business. He can do anything and fix anything, and he often does. He is normally well liked by everyone because he's just so good at his job and can do everyone else's jobs too. He's always on time, dependable, and his schedule never changes much. Without him, the store would always be turned over once every few years. He is the constant factor that brings stability to the store, thus the store has loyal customers and steady business, unlike most other stores. He has probably trained his current managers and bosses, who were probably young pups trained by him once upon a time. In fact, he may have trained several bosses before this current boss. Everyone always praises him who has had the honor of working with him. Everyone from the region knows to call him with questions because they know he's seen it all – and he gets bombarded every day with questions.

Those that are young, worked with him, or his peers always say nothing but positive things about him, and always ask, "Why don't they make Jose a manager? Jeez, that guy knows more than anyone in the district! Look how many people he's trained!"

The bosses cut him as much slack as he wants up to certain points, take him seriously, and consult him on any important matter. When new things, programs, and initiatives come up, they make it a point to get his opinion on it and ask him to do some trainings or be the first to endorse it. He usually tells it how it is and his words carry some weight.

My Jose was the absolute nicest guy in the world.

The Typical Jose will normally tell you this if you ask him why he doesn't want to move up because there's been plenty of openings, he will say, "I tried" or "I'm happy where I'm at" or "I'd probably be a better rep than most of these young pups but it's a young man's game" or "Nah, I don't want the responsibility" or "I don't want to kiss anyone's ass" or "Look at me, I'm Mexican, they'll never allow a Mexican to disrupt the status quo" or "I don't want to move, my house is already paid off" or any number of similar things.

If you gain his trust and speak deeply with him, he'll tell you that he was once a young pup with wild ambitions of grandeur. He'll tell you that he worked really hard and moved up from the lowest part-time position to full-time, but because he didn't have a college education, he kept getting passed over and over by young whipper-snapper, entitled, brown-nosing college grads year after year for that lucrative Assistant Manager position.

Or he may have been a college grad that was an Assistant Manager but could never make it to Store Manager or Sales Manager for one reason or another, mostly because they don't look the part, and now he's what we called a "Lifetime Ass-Man." My old workplace, The Paint Company, was notorious for churning out Typical Joses. But if you delve deeper, he will tell you that he was passed over 7 or 8 times, for one reason or another – he was too Mexican, or Asian, or black, or white, didn't have the right education, he didn't want to kiss ass, upper management was a bunch of a-holes – so he just stopped interviewing and posting for jobs because what's the point. Then he'll tell you sometimes he still thinks about it, but he's old and doesn't want to deal with all the responsibilities, plus his life is set up perfectly where he wants it to be now.

BS.

The #truth is that the human mind is really good at protecting its number one asset – itself. Over the years, it has lied to you to keep you from going off the deep end. It likes comfort. It doesn't want you to be pushed too hard one way or the other. It has convinced you that it was just not meant to be. It uses logic, reasons, blame, denial, and every device in the world to protect you from the real truth. Look, nobody is too old, too Mexican or any other race, too dumb, too stupid, too ignorant, or too poor to be successful. The real truth was that you really didn't believe. You didn't want it bad enough to begin with so you blamed everyone and everything for not getting the results you thought you should have had. You didn't do what was required of you when the going got tough. You just flat out quit.

After 6 years of working my butt off for The Company and not getting where I wanted to go, getting turned down 7 times to be a sales rep, waiting year after year for my dreams to happen to me, I started blaming others for my lack of success and just plain gave up hope.

I became one of those guys who I said I would never be like when I first started working.

When young guys and gals would tell me their dreams and aspirations, I'd shoot them down quickly and say, "Yeah yeah, that's what they all say! I said the same thing five years ago! Do me a favor, shut the hell up, yeah? You don't even how to match paint right now, you don't know squat! Tell me again in 5 years when you're still here like the rest of us!"

I hope nobody listened to this old fart. Sadly, I've actually seen others follow my same path and I didn't do anything about it. The worst was that I may have helped them along that path.

Even when they did give me a shot at being sales rep, after they ran out of excuses and good options, I was already bitten with the Typical Jose bug. I simply just gave up all sports, started drinking heavily, started smoking cigarettes regularly, working for the weekend, didn't care about my diet and got skinny-fat, didn't care about my marriage because I was miserable at work, gave up on climbing the corporate ladder while all my peers moved up and out, gave up on my dreams, sat on my butt all day, lived only to please my wife and kids but couldn't, didn't stay in touch with any of my old friends anymore, didn't talk to my family much either, and started becoming The Typical Jose – dead, just waiting to be buried 50 years down the line.

It would take me eight years of trying to find my way back to who I was when I was All In and successful at everything I did. Massive failures occurred within those eight years, but also some of the best things that ever happened to me. My only regret was that I didn't fail sooner, but you know what they say, the more expensive the lesson, the more you'll remember it. I almost got divorced every single day, had two wonderful sons, lost a young cousin too early, got fired from my job, went into business, failed massively at business a couple of years after, lost all my life savings and my parent's loaned money, had anxiety attacks, thoughts of suicide, got fit and healthy, got back into art again, broke par at golf, learned the most I've ever learned in my life, and found my true calling in life.

You know you're doing something right or you know you've made it when your wife yells at you, "All you want to do is work out! Ever since I've known you, you're always just so competitive and wanna work out all day! You're just crazy about working out all the time! All you do is talk about working out, looking at workout videos, checking yourself out in the mirror, you're just too obsessed and crazy, it's all or nothing with you, it's driving me nuts!"

"Whoa, whoa, whoa! Ever since you've known me? Wow! Really? Did you just say that?" I laughed in amazement. "I didn't even start working out until 3 years ago! It was because you told me I was old and fat, remember? I never touched a single dumb-bell in my life or been to a gym before that! Remember when I got the P90-X workout program to learn how to work out and you bet that I would quit? I did quit after one month because I was not following the diet so I didn't see any noticeable results! I was sore for no goddamn reason. You'd tell me to stop making so much damn noise in the garage so I had to sneak in workouts after the kids went to sleep. Then I came back again with a vengeance because my cousin lost weight on the program, then my buddy lost weight on the program, so I tried it again the way it was designed and went from my heaviest at 160lbs to 135lbs with a six-pack? Then I joined a gym and started doing whatever it took, including waking up at 3AM in the morning every day because you won't let me work out after work because you wanted that time away from the kids! I was too tired after putting the kids to sleep so I couldn't work out at nights so I had to force myself to wake up early every morning even though I was not a morning person! Remember? Wow! You seriously don't remember calling me fat and old and made fun of me? I was always a skinny dude that only played basketball and tennis, did you not remember? Wow! But you know what this means, this means I've made it! It's not an act anymore! This is such a habit now that I've convinced my own wife that this is who I've always been – a work out fanatic! I've made it!"

I was so dedicated and passionate about working out that my own wife thinks I'm just obsessed and crazy. Nobody in their right mind could like something so much could they? They must be crazy. There must be something wrong with me because normal people don't work out this much. This is just an example of working out and being fit, but this applies to everything in life as well. I was crazy about my girlfriend before I married her.

Normal. Now that I know better, I know that normal is actually what is wrong with most people. It's not their fault most of the time. Their parents, the media, and society has taught them that normal is good and normal is safe, that normal is the way in all things. Lies! Most of the time, your goal in life is not to be normal. Normal is too damn pervasive and accepted these days.

"I take care of my kids!" Like Chris Rock said, "What? You want a cookie? You're supposed to, Bleep!"

"I didn't go to jail!"

"I don't want to create more work for myself!"

"I'm not paid enough!"

"I got a C, I didn't fail, yae!"

"I got a job!"

"I made budget!"

You're supposed to! You don't get extra points or cookies for doing what you're supposed to do! Come on, Man! Your goal should be to be more than average, more than normal. Your goal should be to be freaking excellent. Your goal should be to be an expert at whatever you do. Your goal should be to be the absolute freaking best – at your job, at being a husband, wife, son, daughter, brother, sister, or parent, at your business, at your body, at your mind, at being a friend, at sales definitely, and at everything that you do! All In!

"Best not make people think you're crazy, lest they not you," people would always say. Screw that. To be successful in anything, you must be crazy. You must be all in. You must not give two raps about what people think of you. Otherwise, you will put in normal actions, and when you put in normal actions, you get normal results. Fear of what people think about you is just plain dumb. No matter what, you'll be criticized and hated on anyway. The only way to not be criticized is to do nothing and be nothing. In fact, even if you do nothing at all and live in your parents' basement, you'll still be criticized. There's no way around the hate so you might as well do something with your life.

You can't put in normal actions if you hope to achieve anything great in life. Nobody I know has ever been excellent at their jobs, at management, at sales especially, at their business, at fitness, at being a good husband or wife, at being a good parent, at life by putting in normal 9-5 type of work, or only doing exactly what they pay you enough to do, never above or beyond. You have to become so passionate, so dedicated, so obsessive, so crazy, so consistent, and so all in that you convince your own wife or husband that this is who you've always been even though the fact was you were the complete opposite before when they met you. That's when it has become habit and lifestyle. You won't even have to think about it much anymore, it has become you. It is who you are now. That is when you know you've arrived. That is when you have become The One and you did not turn into the Typical Jose.

Chapter 7 #Turths

- Everyone knows a Typical Jose, you may be one
- People tell themselves lies to be comfortable
- People tell you that you can't because they couldn't
- Don't be normal, be All In

Chapter 8: Nobody Will Do Your Pushups For You

Your belief in yourself is all that matters. If you don't believe in yourself and your dreams, then who will? Furthermore, if you don't believe you can do anything, then nobody will. More importantly, it doesn't matter who believes in you - your parents, your family, your friends, or even if everyone in the world believes in you - if you don't believe in yourself, then you will never be able to accomplish anything worthwhile in life.

So you must believe in yourself and your dreams enough to start…today. You never know what tomorrow will bring. Start today. My little brother, Keng, was just here yesterday and gone today. There's an old Hmong saying, Time does not wait for us, but we wait for time. Don't wait for time. Start today. Where ever you are in life. You must start today. With what little resources you might have. Just start today. And if you are like me and you started many times before but failed…start again, today. And believe that this time it will be different. Believe it with all your heart. Everything you ever want depends on it.

Trust me, I know how it FEELS to be dirt poor. I know how it feels to be laughed at. I know how it feels to be embarrassed. I know how it feels to be awkward. I know how it feels to not be taken seriously. I know how it feels to just want to fit in. I know how it feels to be loser and be lost. I know how it feels to be scared. I know how it feels to doubt yourself all the time. I know how it feels to be passed over time and time again. I know how it feels to be disappointed. I know how it feels to be angry and depressed. I know how it feels to want to give up every single day. I certainly know how it feels to wonder if there's ever going to be a light at the end of the tunnel or ask yourself, "Who am I to deserve to live an awesome life? I'm just…" But belief is the first step to getting out of your suffering. You must believe in yourself.

When you don't believe in yourself, when you don't have a dream to follow, when you don't have a definite aim, purpose, or vision, plan, or clue what you want to do in life or in any area of your life…then you just wander around aimlessly like a pinball in a pinball machine, getting knocked around by everyone and everything. It will be by pure luck, pure accident that you get to some semblance of what you thought your life was going to be like. If you actually manage to get there, it would take you years if not decades longer than you expect.

My father-in-law is a walking impressive library of Chinese proverbs. He has seen so much tragedy that he prefers to never talk about the old life in Laos and Thailand after the Vietnam War. Whenever you talk to him about anything about life, you have a tough decision to make, or you're having a hard time with something, he'll have a perfect proverb readily available to share with you. Some will just have you scratching your head at the sheer genius and simplicity of it. I guess you become like this when you've had such a tough life and you want nothing but to seek a simple and peaceful life in Canada. The one proverb that always stuck with me the most was, a plan is like a 100-year shortcut. He explained that if someone doesn't show you the way or you never know where you're going, then most people never get to their destination even if it takes them a hundred years or a lifetime. However, if you have a plan, then it will be like having a map that takes you on the shortcut path and you won't spend your whole life lost like most people. Thanks, Dad, sometimes I do listen.

Since you don't have a plan, you'll be on other peoples' plans. At sales, you'll be on your boss's plan, your co-workers' plans, or your customers' plans – do this, do that, deliver this, deliver that, go here, go there, thank you for all your hard work but we've found someone more qualified. When you come home, you'll be on your wife or husband's plan

– do this, do that, go here, go there, play with the kids, you're not playing with the kids enough, thank you for your hard work, but it's still not enough – and he or she's still unhappy. When you do have a little time for yourself, you'll be on your friends' or family's plans – go here, go there, this place, that place. Before you know it, ten or twenty or God-forbid, your whole life has gone by and you haven't done anything worthwhile for yourself. Then you will truly know suffering…then you die. How do I know all this? Because I've experienced all this first hand.

Furthermore, if people don't run you, then life will run you, guaranteed. Your life will be a series of trying to please others and trying to make everyone happy, then trying to get through problems and circumstances when they arise. Make no doubt about it, problems and circumstances will always arise no matter how careful you are or no matter how safe you try to play it. It's a part of life itself. As far back as I can remember, even in the refugee camps, my father always told me, "Son, make sure do what's required of you to save up, otherwise when it rains, it pours, and you will be destroyed when problems arise. Son, life is full of ups and downs, the trick is take advantage of the ups so you can be ready to deal with the downs." Truer words have never been uttered. You'll just go round and round, getting nowhere, but until you change what you do, the results will be the same. It doesn't matter how long you've been doing it, if you've been doing it the wrong way, you'll always suck. I've known golfers who've played golf for 25 years and can't break 100. I've known people who go to the gym for years and still look the same as if they've just stepped into the gym for the first time. I've known reps that have been doing the same thing for 25 years and sucked for all 25 years. It would be real crazy – insanity – to think that doing the same thing over and over again will produce a different result. You have to get better as you get older because it will never get easier. Otherwise you get stuck. When you get stuck you don't grow. And if you don't grow, you're dead…waiting to be buried many years later.

Life has a funny way of testing you by putting you through the ringers to see if you want something bad enough, to see if you believe in something enough to fight for it, and earn it. Life doesn't give you want, what you wish for, what you pray for, what you think you deserve, it only gives you back what you put in. If it did, everyone would win the lottery. If it did, I would be the best basketball player of all time like Michael Jordan. Some haters are going to say, "Oh, well screw you! You don't know anything about what I've put in! I've put in so much already, there must be another reason or a secret they're not telling us or they must be assholes!" But the #truth is if you put in the work long enough, for a long enough timeline, then the results will come find you because of who you are. You wouldn't need to keep chasing it, it will just come to you. It has no choice. You don't get what you wish for, you get what comes to you when you become that person. Your real decisions, actions, habits, lifestyle, and beliefs are what makes up the person that you are. If they are not aligned with who you say you are, who you pretend to be, who you want others to see, who you wish you are, and who you think you are, then you will not get the success you want.

The best tangible example I know is fitness. You will never be fit if you just want, wish, pretend to work out, say you will work out but don't, and think you work out but don't. Abs don't lie. You can't pay someone else to do the push-ups for you. You can't buy abs. You can't sit on the couch, eat potato chips, and watch TV all the time, and get abs. You can't just know and not believe. You have to believe enough to keep your word, to take massive action, and be All In. Nobody will do push-ups for you.

Chapter 8 #Truths

- Belief in yourself is more important than everyone believing in you
- Start today, wherever you are in life
- You're not alone in suffering
- No purpose, you're like a pinball in a pinball machine
- A plan is like a 100-year shortcut
- If you have no plan, you're on other peoples' plans
- Life will test you to see if you want something bad enough
- Abs don't lie
- You can't pay someone to do your push-ups for you to get muscle

Chapter 9: A Giant Leap of Faith

When an old friend from The Paint Company approached me around the time of Keng's death in 2013, I took a giant leap of faith and immediately joined. I was going to wait until I received my bonus trip award in April 2014 the following year for hitting my numbers again, but I was cheated out of it by the company so I decided to go out in spectacular fashion since there was no use in staying anymore.

And that, Ladies and Gentlemen, was how I got fired from a Fortune 500 company and got labeled as the most dangerous man to ever work for The Paint Company. Me? Little ol' 5'5 and three quarter inches, me? They even put a B.O.L.O. on me to all the stores in the west region. It stands for Be On the Look Out. It's actually law enforcement jargon for someone who is dangerous and must be reported to the police immediately when seen on site. That was the first time anyone has ever gotten a B.O.L.O. from the company apparently, because nobody had ever seen one before. All my friends from the company (and I had a lot) called me up and blew up my phone with text messages calling me BOLO. That's how I got the nickname. But you mean to tell me, that out of the 150 year history of The Freakin' Paint Company, I'm the most dangerous dude to ever walk through their doors? Hmm...big pockets, big potential wrongful termination lawsuit, lots of friends...probably had something to do with it. Usual scare tactic used by them, flexing their big muscles against the little guy. What they didn't know was that I was already All In on my future and they were already in my rear-view mirror. I could care less. I sold off all my stocks pretty quickly. All Out with nothing on my conscience even if the stock price did quickly double. My wife was obviously upset at how I went out, but I had to do what I had to do. I was not going to wait on my dreams one second longer. I was All In, even though I had no clue how I was going to do it. It worked out because I was able to survive on the unemployment money for a bit while I worked on the business. Everyone said I was crazy – my friends, my co-workers, my parents, my brother, and my very own wife.

They said to me, "Now you do it? You couldn't have done it 5 years ago? Or waited till your kids are older and in kindergarten when your wife can go get a job and support you guys?"

"You had a cush job! One of the best reps in the company, clocking in over six figures, making plenty of money to support your family without your wife working, you had a company car, gas card, expense account, and you could drink, smoke, and play golf on the company. Are you crazy?"

Yes, because I wasn't about to do the same thing over and over and expect a different result each time. I had done enough of that. That is the definition of insanity as Albert Einstein famously quoted. Call me crazy but I wasn't about to work another 10 more years of this; wandering aimlessly in Southern California, having no savings account, doing something I absolutely hated, dragging myself out of bed every day, suffering through traffic to work, waiting for the clock to strike 5 P.M., and fighting traffic all the way home, just so I could sit my ass on the couch, drink a half a bottle of Jack, watch my favorite TV shows, and then crawl to bed not caring whether I wake up or not. My couch had a perfect indentation of my butt in it. I was driving my wife absolutely miserable because of my own misery. I couldn't enjoy being with my kids. I became a cynical asshole. I had no energy. I was getting fat and lazy, with chronic pain in my back and neck. I had bad habits everyday like smoking cigarettes, drinking alcohol, eating fast food and junk food, energy drinks, sugary sodas, video games, gambling, and I couldn't wait until the weekend just so I could sleep in and recover so that I could have the energy to repeat the week over again. Life is movement and I was dead, just waiting to be buried years later.

So yes, I was crazy, because I'd rather die right now instead of having to go through another 30 or 40 more years of this mediocre life. Or maybe I just woke up to work on my dreams, unlike most people who will sleep and dream their lives away. Most likely, thought, I just didn't want to be stuck in nightmare until I finally wake up at 80 or 90 years of age and then regret all the things I didn't do in life.

But because of Keng, I took a chance. I didn't know how. I didn't know if it was even the right decision. I didn't know if it was the right timing. I didn't have a lot of money. I was scared out of my mind, but I knew I had to do something…anything. So I just did it! For me this was the hardest part…the starting part. I once promised myself that in 5 years after working for The Company, I was going to start my own business. Then 5 years turned into 10 years. Then 10 years was turning into 15 years. And in my heart and in my soul, I knew it was never going to happen, until Keng's death propelled me into massive chaotic action. I wish I wasn't All In all the time, all or nothing, do or die, but for me, this is how I work the best…and I truly believe, this is what it's like for most people as well. It would obviously be easier and less disruptive if I had the discipline and skill to create and build the business slowly, methodically, and strategically. Unfortunately, for me and for most people, I didn't have the discipline, the skills, the knowledge, or the wisdom. The ol' chicken or the egg, I guess. The good news is, all you really need is crazy purpose and action. The rest will come if you are truly All In.

So I borrowed a lot of money from my parents to start the business. I bit the bullet and went back on welfare and Medi-cal. My family hasn't been on welfare since we came to America 27 years ago! We promised ourselves that we will never be on Welfare again. But you have to do what you have to do, so I swallowed my very last bit of pride, sucked it up, stopped playing golf, got to the business of struggling, lived off Unemployment money, worked my butt off, slept only 3 hours a day, had anxiety attacks, and failed miserably because I didn't believe in myself…enough. I still had fear that I was going to fail. I doubted myself that I could do it by myself so that's why I got a partner. I believed in myself to start but I just didn't believe in myself ENOUGH to succeed and because of that, I almost single handedly brought everything and everyone close to me down with the flames.

I almost went bankrupt. I lost all my savings and most of my retirement money. If you've ever lost a lot of money, you understand my pain. I also spent all my parents' live savings. Twenty-seven years in America, saving every single dime since we came here, and I lost it all in one year…in spectacular fashion! My parents were the typical hard working Asian parents. They hate spending, they loved saving. For a while in America, the only time we got to eat out was when my brother and I got straight A's in school. That was the only time my dad would take us out to treat my brother and I for Three Taco deals at Taco Bell. We had to get all A's for that. For several years, I watched my brother eat tacos in tears because I just couldn't get straight A's due being so far behind in school. Sometimes he would purposely not finish each taco and leave a bite or two in the wrapper for me to clean up when Dad wasn't looking. Dad didn't look a lot of times. We thought we were pretty smart or Dad was just oblivious. I know now that Dad took me all the time to see my brother eat tacos because he wanted me to use that dreadful feeling as motivation and to pick up scraps from my brother while he pretended not to know what was going on. I'm sure now that he didn't enjoy doing that to me, but a real man does what he has to do for his family. My parents worked every single type of job and saved every single penny that wasn't absolutely necessary for the family to spend. Because my brother knew how hard they worked and how hard they saved, now he's pissed at me as well – figuring that I must have manipulated my parents' love to finagle them out of their life savings. I hope you'll never have to find out, but if you've ever lost other people's money, you'll know that it's one of the worst feelings in the world, especially if it's with your own hard working parents.

I put my wife through hell with my stubbornness, even as she supported me the whole way. There were numerous times when we didn't know how we were going to pay next month's mortgage. Even though she'd threaten to divorce me every other day, she never pulled the trigger and stuck with me through it all. We learned to live below our means, struggle and grow together, take inventory of what was truly important, make tough decisions, and become grateful again. She was a champ and will always be my champ. A true keeper. She wasn't like the other girls I grew up with or were friends with. These girls were all looking for a man that was already made, dressed well, had a great job or business, and drove a nice car. When they didn't find one, they all complained that all the good ones were taken. They didn't want to take responsibility and put in the work for picking up a nice young boy with potential, grooming him, turning him into a great finished product, and staying loyal to him, like she did me. Real men are loyal. You have to be loyal to those who are loyal to you. She saw something in me when I was nothing and knew nothing. Because of her strength and stubbornness, I grew into the person I am today. It wasn't always roses, but I would not be as strong now if not for her. She will always be The One.

Somehow l was still alive. From that, I know...nay...I believe now that what doesn't kill you truly makes you stronger. But damn did I spend many a night awake looking for an answer, not being able to go to sleep, suffering through anxiety attacks and contemplating suicide. After the pain subsided, the dust had settled, my dad kicked my ass, and the legal matters were over, I was able to sit back and reflect upon all that transpired, and the result is this book. People would often ask me if I regret doing what I did. I always said, yes, I regret not doing it sooner.

Without question, if you ask me the one reason why I failed, why I didn't succeed, it was because I didn't believe in myself. If I did, I wouldn't have needed a partner in the first place. I would have done it by myself. If I did, I would have gotten my own C-33 license, which was a stupid fear I had in my head that I anguished over for years because everyone said it was so hard. In the end, it was actually really freakin' easy – on my test, I was the first person done and passed with flying colors. If I did, I would have done things differently. If I did, I would have had more conviction in my business dealings and all my communications. If I did, I would have been so much more aggressive. If I did, I would have closed all my sales opportunities – I know it. If I did, I wouldn't have quit. If I did, I might have actually been successful and that probably would have been the worst mistake of my life. Why? Because I would have never learned this lesson that I will forever keep within me. I would never be this strong and I would never know what I know now. I would still be a contractor, doing something that I absolutely dreaded. Worse, I would probably have been divorced by now. Worse yet, I would probably still not see my kids much from the stressful workload and the divorce. But most importantly, I would never have found my true calling in life – inspirational speaking.

Speaking of inspirational speaking, when I decided to become an inspirational speaker, did you think that the clouds parted and a ray of light purposefully shined down on me while Rafiki lifted me into the air to receive my destiny, like in *The Lion King* movie? No. I wish. I just took a giant leap of faith, even after three failed businesses back to back. For no other reason than it just felt right, in my heart and in my soul. It was inspiring to me. There wasn't as much fear when I thought about it. Thinking about it made me feel good. It felt like the right thing to do. It was also for a good cause. Sales is what I'm really freaking good at because of necessity, but inspirational speaking – even though I suck at it right now – is what I was born to do. So I did. It wasn't for the money this time. It was a conscience decision to never quit doing it until I succeed even if I never get paid a single cent. Most of the time you just don't know, you just do it. You just commit to something, do what you say you're going to do, and make sure you give it everything you got and more... All In.

As I got better in sales and started walking the stage year after year, many young sales reps would come up to me and ask me, "Hey, Bolo, I want to be like you but how do I know what segment I should go into? Do I choose Commercial? Or Property Management? Or Residential Repaint? Or Industrial? Or if sales is even what I want to do?"

I always just tilt my head and reply, You tell me... better yet, you tell yourself. They would usually follow up with, But I don't know.

Then I tell them to take a giant leap of faith and be All In.

I always tell them that the ultimate goal in life is to find out what you want in life. But that may never happen for most people. Michael Jordan was born to play basketball. Tiger Woods was born to play golf. Tony Robbins was born to be the ultimate Inspirational Speaker. MLK was born to fight for civil rights. And so on and so forth. But again, that's the very very very few lucky ones.

However, the consolation prize is finding out what you DON'T want in life. Most times, like I did with sales and contracting, you just grab your balls, say F-It, and take a giant leap of faith. You just commit to be really good at it and give it your all. Be All In and see what happens! Maybe when you try enough times at finding out what you don't want, just maybe, you'll end up finding what you DO want in life.

So don't get too attached to the results. The real prize is the actualization of yourself. Learn to enjoy the process. Because life *is* a process. These days I love trying out new stuff and enjoying the process along the way. I've got a formula now, it's really simple: All In.

By the way, did you think I knew how to write a book? No. As you can probably tell by all the grammatical errors and run-on sentences. But I needed to share Keng's story, so that others who are in the same shoes I was in could find reprieve from all the unnecessary suffering that I knew so well. I turned it into a sales book because I wanted to make a difference at Behr. They are the professional family I never had. That's the way a company should be. They took me in...I mean, they almost literally took me in off the streets. That made it easy for me to be All In to Win with them. But again, it just felt right. It felt good. It was also a good cause. Thinking about it inspires me. There's very little fear or doubt when I think about it. And most assuredly, I didn't know where to begin. I don't even read much myself, except like most people - emails, magazines, Facebook posts, and stuff like that. I didn't know what genre this book would belong to. I didn't have any friends that were authors. I just started typing...to clear my soul. I didn't know where it was going to go. I could give a rat's ass about the results. I just had to let it out and trust in the universe that things will work out when I do what feels right in my heart. All In. At the same time, the act of writing itself was cathartic and slowly the pain and suffering disappeared. I took a giant leap of faith that I was doing the right thing and that was enough even if this book didn't sell a single copy. It still had to be written because Keng's story had to be told.

Sometimes in life, you just have to breathe real deep, hold your nose, close your eyes, grab your balls, jump in with both feet, and hope for the best and trust that things will work themselves out as they always do when you go All In. Fear is just in your head. Failure is never final unless you give up. Success takes courage.

Sometimes...when it feels good in your heart, right in your mind, and inspiring to your soul, you just have push all your chips in and...take a giant leap of faith.

Chapter 9 #Truths

- There's never a perfect time to start anything
- It's insanity to do the same thing over and over and expect a different result each time
- You must wake up to work on your dreams
- You don't have to have all the answers, just start
- Massive purpose and action is more important than all the skills, knowledge, and wisdom
- What doesn't kill you makes you stronger
- You don't need to have all the answers, you just need to believe
- Sometimes you just need to take a gaint leap of faith and jump in
- Success takes courage

Chapter 10: One Mountain a Day

"Wake up, Son, we have to go right now, the Vietnamese are coming!"

My earliest memory was my mom waking me up in the middle of the night in a panic. Even though it was dark, I could see and hear the shadows of my frantic uncles and aunts grabbing things and stuffing things into other things. I didn't know it then, but we had to flee the village that we were in and make our way to the closest safe village because the Vietcong were getting closer. I remember not having any shoes on that night. In fact, I didn't have shoes most of my young life. Walking through the jungle trails, I remember looking down at my little bare feet while struggling to keep up with Mom. She was carrying my brother on her back with a small bag of salvaged rice, some clothes, and other belongings on her front. I saw and felt my tiny toes touching jungle leaves and certain brownish, round, hard nuts. I still remember it so vividly nowadays, and still have recurring dreams of this same scene on many a night. Later, I described that dream to my mom and asked her what those brown nuts might have been. She was so surprised that I could remember that night. She said I was only about three years old when we fled. We marched in single file on an old worn dirt trail – made even more slippery by the torrential rain, careful not to stray even a foot off so we wouldn't step on the landmines littered everywhere – into the jungle, over mountains, and down hills for several days and nights. Mom told me that those nuts were water chestnuts and they were plentiful in certain parts back then.

On that night, Mom had my brother strapped on her back with a Hmong-style baby sling carrier while I held her hand from behind, trying my very best to keep up. She said it was one of the longest and scariest nights of her life. My dad had already went ahead first with my grandparents to make sure the trail was safe, then he was supposed to come back and get us, but the Vietnamese were spotted earlier than expected so we had to flee before he could come back. I was tired from waking up in the middle of the night and wanted to be carried by Mom as well. She told me that I had to help Mommy and I was a big strong boy now so I could walk by myself, so I did for certain periods, but other times, when my little bare feet were too pricked by thorns and branches, she'd have to carry me too. To this day, tears still run down her face when she describes the many times we'd all tumble over together – dripping wet, hungry, sore, covered in mud, cuts, and scrapes – with both my brother and I crying right along with her.

"How did you do it, Mom?" I would always ask her.

"One mountain a day, Son," she would always say.

Now that I'm older, I finally know what she meant. She wasn't just being literal. She would always say that to me but I never quite fully understood until after I had struggled enough.

"One mountain a day, Son. It always seems impossible when you look at the whole journey and all those mountains in front of you, but if you say to yourself, "I just need to make it over this one mountain today," then everyone can do it. Everyone can climb just one mountain a day. Everyone can survive just one day. Then tomorrow, another mountain, another day. That's how survivors survive, Son, that's the secret to surviving, one mountain a day."

Through it all – the constant fleeing, the years of refugee camp life, and all the starting over – I learned an important lesson: even though we were so poor and experienced so much hardship, I was happy and grateful because I knew I had people that loved me more than anything else in the whole world.

Through tremendous struggle, I learned that you get exactly the things you need right when you need them. I would argue I didn't need to be almost bankrupt but I guess in retrospect, I needed the lesson. I wouldn't have learned what I know now if I didn't go through what I went through then. The more expensive the lesson, the more you'll learn from it, I guess. I used to look down upon people who have failed even though they are so successful currently. I'd hate on them, throw shade as the kids say these days, and say stupid things like, "Yeah, but he failed at this and that, shoot, he's a loser!" I'd tell friends of mine, "Why should I listen to you about marriage, you're divorced!" My God, was I ever wrong about anything. You could learn from other people's failures and you will definitely learn more from failures than success. All the combined successes in my life could not amount to the lessons I've learned through one massive failure.

Failures, difficulties, and struggles are necessary for growth and a grateful life. Nobody can be successful all the time or be happy all the time. If they say they are, they are lying to you or lying to themselves. If you only succeed and never struggle, it's just physiologically impossible for you to stay grounded and appreciate life. It's like too much of a drug, your body gets used to it, and it becomes incredibly tough to enjoy life.

Like my father, the farmer, would always say, "Too much sunshine and there will be drought, you need some rain to appreciate the sun. Too much rain and there will be floods. Either way, everything dies. You need some struggles, otherwise you become spoiled like my strawberries."

If you live in a state of comfort all the time, you don't grow, you don't get better. It's true for personal growth as it is for relationships, business, fitness, or almost anything else in life. I always go back to working out because it is the most tangible thing I can compare to your mind and to life itself. Your mind is a like a muscle, it must be exercised for it to grow. The same goes for your life. In life, you must struggle in order for you to grow just like when you work out. You must fatigue your muscles to exhaustion and break down the fibers so that they can rebuild themselves bigger and stronger. The more you do this, the faster your muscles will grow. You subject them to this stress every day and they will grow bigger and stronger every day. It's actually quite simple fundamentally. You have to learn to enjoy the soreness or at the very least, get used to it where it doesn't impede you but help you.

When I first started on my fitness journey, I failed massively initially, that's why now I not only know what to do, but what not to do. I did as all amateurs did when starting something new. I didn't believe. I wasn't fully committed. I hated every step of the way. I was looking for excuses everywhere. I didn't read, ask questions, or do any research. I didn't follow the system the way it was designed. I didn't have a plan. I was extremely frugal with the things that mattered which were my diet and knowledge. I only did the exercises when I felt like it and when I wasn't too sore. I still ate like a pig. And when I didn't see fast results, I quit.

I was destined to fail miserably because I wasn't all in. I'm glad I did fail because I would never have known what not to do and now my conviction of what to do correctly is stronger than ever. The same goes for being a horrible store manager and then working my way to becoming a great manager. The same also goes to being such a poor sales rep, then going All In into being one of the best reps ever. From massive failure, I realized fear was just fear and failure is sometimes a good thing, and I learned to grow from it. In life, just like your muscles, if you're not growing, you're dying. When companies don't grow anymore, they start dying too. If you don't find a way to break through your plateaus, one mountain a day, if you don't change, if you don't grow, if you can't learn new tricks, that's when you become old and you start dying, just waiting to be buried later.

That is why I am so confident in the skills I've developed, because I had to earn them through decades of struggle. One mountain a day. The same way some of these fit guys walk around without a shirt on, flexing and staring at their muscles all the time – they worked hard for it, they earned it. Yeah, they could probably be a little less outwardly obvious about it, as not to offend certain people, but that's really the offended person's issue if you really think about it. Many people who don't know me well have told me that I am just a rich spoiled arrogant Korean kid. And I'm not even Korean. They think I've got some baseless arrogance and entitlement probably due to my parents but they're so wrong on so many levels.

I was never meant to be a sales rep. It was probably the most opposite career choice for a guy that was naturally a shy, introverted immigrant who was deathly afraid of rejection due to early conditioning by my elders. People who never knew me before I became a successful rep would have never thought I was so introverted before. This persona I've created for myself to be able to work in sales and excel in it has served its purpose very well. I'm extremely confident now because it took me over two years, one mountain a day, to just learn how to look at people in the eye when I started working fulltime after college. It took me years of hard work, every single day, one mountain a day, fighting through all my fears, making a ton of mistakes, struggling, overcoming, growing, and methodically getting better to this point. I've put in the work so I walk around confident in my abilities to take on any situation and succeed. My confidence and unwillingness to settle for mediocrity for myself or the people I work with has made many people resent me. I used to stress over other people's opinion of me, but these days, I have no room for any of that. The way I see it, as a sales rep, if you're not constantly learning every day, not constantly trying to get better every day, and not constantly pushing yourself to failure each day, then you'll never be a great sales rep.

I learned that you have to fail to truly succeed. All successful people in the world have failed and will never be immune to failure, but they succeed more because they believe this fact and don't fear it. Without failure, you'll never really know what you are capable of. The more spectacular the failure, the more you will learn from it as long as it doesn't kill you. As the saying goes, what doesn't kill you makes you stronger. Before it just sounded good, now I know what that truly means. Those who have never failed, have never set the bar high enough so they either just never tried at all or they easily succeeded. I'm not saying people who have never failed didn't work hard. I'm saying they could have succeeded much more had they raised the bar higher, set their goals higher, dreamed bigger, took more chances, failed as many times as it takes, learned, got back up, and then succeeded beyond their wildest dreams. That is why there are many people who come from poor and tough backgrounds that have become some of the most successful people in the world. When they survive things like extreme poverty, conflicts, struggles, war, and brutal upbringings, they believe they can survive almost anything else so they persevere until they succeed using the skills, knowledge, lessons, and experience they gathered along the way. This is where long term success comes in. This is where success becomes a habit. This is where the rich get richer and the poor get poorer. This is where luck turns into skill. At some point – if you're not a hater - you just have to tip your hat to them and admit that they deserve it. See, the poor get poorer because they've never learned what it took to be successful. Even if they win the lottery, most lose it all and more. They don't have the skills, knowledge, lessons, and experiences to be successful and keep being successful because they've always either quit every single time something hard comes along, just steer clear, take the path of least resistance, or just do enough to get by. They keep doing that over and over for the rest of their lives until something tragedy forces them to change, if ever. The habitual successful person has struggled, persevered, and overcame so much that when another tough situation arises, he or she believes they can do it, and they go out and do whatever it takes to get it done. As they get older, things don't get any easier for them. They will realize that they just have to get stronger, smarter, wiser, and better. They will know it will take more than normal things like fear, doubt, getting fired, quitting a job, losing a business, losing your house, starting over, and failure to kill them because they have survived way worse. They know that everyone alive is a survivor, but they also know that eventually we will all run out of time. Nobody is getting out of this rock alive so they might has well use the time they have to do more than just survive – they might as well do something great even if they fail in the process. Even if they do fail, they will understand that failing is a part of life; in fact, they know they can fail at just about anything else so they might as well not fear failing at the things they want to do. They will find out for themselves - after looking outside for everything – that everything was inside them to begin with. They will believe that they have all that it takes within themselves to be successful, no matter how old they are, how young they are, how poor they are, how uneducated they are, or how much they have lost before.

Like my parents right after the war ended. The U.S. had just pulled out of the Vietnam War. Chaos, confusion, fear, and the worst horrors covered the population like napalm. If you weren't the few registered fighters that was immediately within the extraction zones, you were left behind. The hundreds of thousands of Hmong people left behind were left to fend for themselves. The communist Viet Cong and Pathet Lao were coming after us for helping the U.S. during the war. Many perished by way of land mines, capture, injury, gunfire, disease, starvation, and drowning in the crossing of the Mekong River into Thailand from Laos. My dad had to make many trips back into Laos to get the majority of our family to safety, risking death each time. My mom would often talk about having to survive on roots of certain trees for weeks. They would have to boil those roots for a long time to get the acidity and bitterness out. The roots had minimal nutrients but it was better than dying. The only protein came from bugs and critters, maybe a lucky small quail, frog, or a heavenly sent small fresh water crab from a mountain stream. What little meat was had, the elders would chew it up in their mouths to taste the juices, pretend they are really eating it, and then spit it out for the young kids to eat the actual meat. Second-hand meat eating is better than no meat. One mountain a day. Because my brother was always sick and had no appetite, my mom remembered having to breast feed most of my cousins. One mountain a day. Then if you and your family were lucky, you would be settled in a Refugee Camp in Thailand where you'll basically camp out and eat dried sardines and rice for a decade or two. One mountain a day. At some point, my parents believed they are survivors and it will take much more than that to kill them because no matter what is thrown at them, they will survive it. One mountain a day.

I will let you know, you'll get no sympathy from these survivors if you wake up at ten or eleven AM, come to their farm in your car with your kids, say you and your kids are hungry, and beg them to give you fruits and vegetables because my parents are apparently so lucky and well off. They don't have any sympathy for you because they know you are more capable than you believe, you're just lazy. You must do more than survive, you're already good at that if you're reading this book, so do more, be all in, and thrive. And if you're struggling right now, you're where I was, crawling on the bottom of the floor of the deepest, darkest pits of hell right now, and you're wondering how you're ever going to make it out alive...you just have to make it one mountain a day.

Chapter 10 #Truths

- It doesn't matter how poor you are, if you are loved as a kid, you were happy
- You get what you need when you really need them
- You'll learn more from one massive failure than all your successes combined
- Struggle is necessary for growth
- Your mind must be exercised to grow like your muscles
- If you're not growing, you're dying
- Every successful person has failed or they're lying
- What doesn't kill you makes you stronger
- It takes a lot more than you think to kill you
- You're already good at surviving, now thrive
- One mountain a day.

HWO members

From left to right: Ice, Wizard, Master Angle, Silk, Ace, center – Spider

Chapter 11: State

Sometimes you don't know how to believe. That's fine. Sometimes you just have to take a giant leap of faith like our original Hmong tennis team did, and made history. Our tennis team believed in themselves enough to start playing tennis even though they've never picked up a racket until they got to High School. This team produced 3 class valedictorians in a five year span. This team won a lot. We won so much, they made our coach, Coach Jay Marchant, The Coach of the Decade for the whole North State of California. He even said we inspired him to follow his dreams of becoming a principal instead of just coaching his entire life. This team went on to become the first and only boys team in the 80 plus year history of Willows High School to make it to the State Championships.

It may not seem like a big deal, but considering what we had to go through and the fact that it was basically an all-Hmong team, it was a huge deal. The only boys team to ever come from the school! That's why I still hold a little resentment that the school and the principal never even announced it publicly over the intercom to all the students as would normally be done for any other team for far lesser achievements such as just making it to league or sections.

You mean to tell me that, in 80 plus years since the school was established, there had been some really good wrestling teams, football teams, basketball teams, track teams, baseball teams, with kids who had been playing their respective sport since they were really young in grade school, with the best equipment and coaches...and THIS TEAM is the ONLY team that went to state? This team, made up of a bunch of short little Hmong kids? Who went through so much poverty? Who were ridiculed growing up? Who were never given a chance in life? Who never even picked up a racket until they got to High School? Who got their $15 racquets from Wal-Mart to compete against other kids with hundred dollar rackets? Who used the same shoes from basketball and other sports to play tennis that they bought from Payless Shoes years ago? If you looked at some of our old pictures of the tennis team, all our shoes were basketball shoes that we've worn for several years. I remember most of my uncles and aunts wouldn't even let my cousins come out and play with my brother and I because they just didn't understand the idea behind extra-curricular activities. They feared the worst, and they thought sports was just a waste of time or an excuse to gang-bang. It was only until they saw how my brother and I were the top in our classes, getting recognition and awards, and we weren't getting into trouble, that they realized this was a way for their kids to do something positive and stay out of trouble as well. It worked, as we found the competitiveness and will to win that was present all along in all of us. From there, losing was not an option. We finally had a chance to win at something in life.

It all started with me. My brother and I were the first and only Hmong people to start playing organized Little League baseball when I was in the fifth grade and my brother in the third grade. Whatever I did, naturally my brother followed. I competed my absolute best at baseball, the main sport of the white kids in town. I gave up soccer and pursued basketball as well because soccer just wasn't cool. Football was out of the question because my parents wouldn't let me play out of fear that I'd get my bones broken. For a while, I had thought that if I also played football, I'd get more respect from the locals. There wasn't much to do in the small town. Most of the older Hmong men, including all my uncles and my dad, would go play volleyball in the late afternoons at the local Willows Intermediate School almost every day because it was free and they had a lot of free time. Of course, the kids would tag along and play basketball on the many adjacent courts. Through the sheer amount of year-round practice, we all got very good at basketball. We ruled the playgrounds and forged teamwork and competitive spirit. Every other sport was far too expensive for Hmong people. I competed well considering I only played baseball during the season – never able to afford the batting cages and never having anyone to play with, practice with, or learn from until baseball season starts again. In fact, I was one of the better players at my age playing every year until high school.

During my freshmen year, I was the starting point guard on the freshmen basketball team where Coach Jay Marchant of the varsity basketball team saw me in action and thought he could use my speed in tennis, as he was also the tennis coach. It was difficult recruiting good athletes for the tennis team because most of the kids with athletic ability preferred to play the popular hometown sports of football, basketball, and baseball respectively every year. I initially told Coach that I wasn't interested, telling him I was a baseball player. After basketball season, it was baseball season, or depending on your spring sport of choice, tennis and track season as well. I went to try out for the JV baseball team as all freshmen and sophomores would have to do. Much to my dismay, the JV baseball coach made me pick up bats and balls while all the rest of the kids – all white except for one popular Chinese boy – got to practice, bat, field, and run drills. If there was actually time to practice, I'd be dead last, behind notoriously and historically bad players since Little League. I made a complaint to one of the players I grew up playing with to confirm that I was not the worst player on the team, but the coach never listened to him either. After one of the last practices before the end of try-outs, when the coach asked me to pick up bats and balls again, I just stared at him to make sure he and I both knew what was going on, shook my head, turned around, and walked home, with him yelling behind at me all sorts of curse words and racist remarks. I didn't even bother to make all of it out. I had already heard them all. That was the last time I ever touched a baseball bat.

The next day, after school, I walked over to the tennis courts and told Coach Marchant I was done with baseball and I was all in with tennis if he would consider letting me join the tennis team. He told me to go buy a tennis racquet and I would be on the team. I asked my dad to take me to Wal-Mart and he bought me the cheapest racquet we could find for about $15 including tax. It was pink and orange, heavy, had an oversized head, and a short little handle to add insult to my already short limbs. I swear to God this was the reason why I never learned how to serve in my whole high school tennis career.

It was the beginning of a rocky, yet mutually respectful relationship. I never liked Coach as I was always suspicious of most white people. I don't think he ever liked my attitude and aloof demeanor. Although I never liked him because I believed he considered me only as a means to an end and I always knew he thought of me in the same manner, but I respected and admired him tremendously. Coach Marchant was the most athletic, tall, handsome, fun-loving, womanizing, easy-talking, story-telling, and joke-cracking person I've ever known in my life. He was a natural salesman and leader. People just gravitated to him. You can't help but like the guy upon meeting him. I always remembered some of the "rules" he and the team used to tell. The most memorable was "Rule #1: Always look good." I remember Coach would always joke that our team may not be able to help it if we're not good, but there's no excuse for not looking good! This rule would guide me later on in my sales career and life. I would often try to model his personality in my early sales transactions.

After learning the rules of the game and how to play it, I slowly moved up from number 9 to number 6 by the end of the season, relying entirely on my speed and tapping the ball to the backhands of my opponent with my short, oversized racquet and waiting for them to make mistakes. My sophomore year went about the same way, but every day I was getting better at school, basketball, and tennis. I moved up to number 5 at the end of tennis season – we had a pretty good team with an excellent exchange student from Mexico being the number one player.

Junior year was when things started changing due to the arrival of my brother as a freshmen in high school. Varsity basketball was a challenge as I rarely came off the bench behind the seniors, even though they got destroyed in practice and on the playgrounds. However, organized basketball with influential parents and players who had been playing in the same offense for years were too much for me to ever get real playing time. The best thing was that The Lee Brothers were reunited during tennis season – he was number 8 and I was number 5 – all the while we still looked closely, learned quickly, paid attention, and bided our time. We had a lot of time to bond and strategize about what we needed to do to make a name for ourselves, our cousins, and our people.

After one away tennis game, while traveling back home in the school van, my brother and I had a quiet conversation in the back about who amongst our people we could look up to and emulate. There were none. We named some older Hmong cousins and friends, but they didn't fit the bill. They were either really good at sports but could barely finish high school or they were all in gangs. My brother told me that since I was the oldest, I might as well be the hero that the younger cousins could look up to. Reluctantly, after thinking about it, I took a deep breath and took a giant leap of faith.

We started messing around with what the purpose of this new endeavor would look like. My brother said he would support me and help recruit the cousins to our cause. We dared to believe that we could be something more than FOBs, losers, or gang-bangers. There was another option – we could create and become something great. If you look around and find no hero, maybe you might want to look in the mirror.

How did we do it?

We did it because we believed in ourselves. Even though we were so fearful and uncertain, we dared to believe that we could be more than gangsters, losers, and good-for-nothing commie gooks. When my younger cousins, TC, Migo, and Mong came on board as freshmen, my brother was a sophomore, and I was a senior – we became a full team. We were a whole basketball team and pretty much a whole tennis team. We proceeded to call ourselves HWO. Hmong World Outlaws. It was a play on the fact that we felt like we didn't belong to any group – white or Hmong. We even had nicknames for each of us, Master Angle, Ace, Silk, Ice, and Wizard. Our goal was to dominate in school, basketball, and tennis, and be an example to all the many more younger Hmong cousins – boys and girls included – who were yet to enter high school and would be needing heroes to look up to. Everyone laughed at us and mocked us that we were just a fake, pretentious wannabe gang with a name stolen from a WWE pro wrestling group. Everyone laughed, except for us.

Because I had a chip on my shoulder, our group had a chip on our shoulders and we dared to prove to everyone that we were as good if not better than anyone or anything they threw at us. That senior year in basketball, Coach Marchant was replaced with an ex-Chico State basketball standout as the new coach. He was a stranger and didn't have any allegiances to the town. He was tough, strict, and didn't care about anyone or anything else other than winning games, although we weren't very good and we didn't do much winning. I was the best basketball player on the team, the starting senior point-guard. The majority of the team were juniors with few seniors returning as most couldn't make the cut during their prior junior year and never returned to basketball. The thing that stuck with me the most was our first and last league playoff game against Corning. Coach brought up my brother, a sophomore, from the JV basketball team to back me up as point guard in the hope of a fighting chance against our opponent. I got off to a hot start until they started collapsing in the middle and daring me to shoot from outside – they had scouted me out prior – because I couldn't shoot a lick in high school. I always just relied on speed and ball-handling to get to the basket for layups. When I ran out of gas, our coach substituted my brother in for me instead of the other two white junior point guards on the team. They were part of the inner circle of kids from the inner circle of parents of our town. I'm getting better these days, but for a very long time, it still burns me to remember seeing and hearing all the white parents on our same team booing my brother as he went into the game to replace me. I made it a point to turn around and take in all their red twisted faces, white-knuckle raised fists, pointed fingers, and gaping hate-spewing mouths so that when I eventually make it, I would know exactly who to thank. From there, our will was broken and the game was pretty much over. It didn't matter anymore to me anyway. We got dunked on and the game turned out to be a blowout. At the end, I received MVP of the team and All-League honors, but the season was largely a disappointment. Coach also got fired a season later; athough, I suspect it was a mutual agreement.

Tennis season couldn't come quick enough. This was where I would finally get to play with all my cousins, not be an outsider on a team my whole life, and go out the way I wanted and planned. Four more younger cousins, Pan, Long, Tou, and Da, who were still in eighth grade came every day after school to practice with us too, especially during the summer. Coach Marchant saw an opportunity. He would open up a summer tennis camp where all of us including the little ones in junior high could come play tennis, then Coach would open up the swimming pool afterward and we'd just have the best time of our lives. This would soon prove to be very instrumental in making history when the majority of the little cousins did get into high school two years later. It was so much fun that year and they all got very good at tennis during those formative summers. I moved up so many spots from number 5 all the way to number 1, playing all the top players of other teams who were at least a level or two better than me. I did very well – beating all but 3 of the top players in the league who were almost semi-pro – because I wanted to teach my boys how to compete and how to not give up. I was very hard on them, but especially harder on myself, holding everyone to a very high standard.

We pushed each other hard every day on the courts. We hung out together, ate together, and played together every single day. We didn't feel sorry for ourselves. We just believed and competed. You didn't want to lose because you would never hear the end of it, in school or in sports. We tried to destroy each other in fact, because we knew that it would not kill anyone. We had been through way too much already. Our opponents started to fear us and complained about us because we began obliterating all the teams in our league – showing no mercy, making the other kids cry. For us, it wasn't about just merely winning, it was about relishing the chance to finally make a statement. We even had a bagel count going. A bagel is when you beat somebody six to zero, or you get a big fat zero yourself. In high school tennis, to win you have to beat your opponent two out of three sets of six games each set. In professional tennis, it's three out of five sets for men. For us, we'd try to beat opponents 6-0, 6-0 – a double-bagel – every time in the fastest way possible…the best way to win. We all wanted to be the first man to double-bagel our opponent so we could come back and watch the others with the biggest smiles on our faces. This was the greatest time of their lives for many of the team members. This was when they weren't looked down upon. They weren't perpetual losers. They had freedom from their traditional parents. This was their chance to finally get out and see other towns. This was when they started to believe in themselves. For most of us, this was the first time that we found out what winning felt like.

After I graduated high school, my brother took over as the leader of the team, pushing everyone – although in a less verbal and emotional manner – and continuing to dominate all the other schools in the league. Coach Marchant was able to get a sponsorship from the USTA (United

States Tennis Association). The team got brand new uniforms, tennis racquets and bags, a new ball machine, and a boatload of Gatorade, the most prized of them all.

Two years after I left, our team made history, despite of it all. They beat everyone at the League Playoffs and beat a school four times their size at the Sectionals to make it to the State Championships. It didn't matter that this was the first time most of them got to go anywhere past Sacramento, that their parents had no clue what was going on, that the other opponents cheered for them more than their own school and hometown, that they were so overwhelmed by the whole experience of going to such a big place like Stanford and playing against kids who knew they belonged, or the fact that they got completely destroyed in spectacular fashion, all that mattered was that they knew what winning felt like.

It was the first time in the history of Willows High School that a boys team made it to State. The town newspaper wrote a story about our tennis team, but the school itself pretended nothing happened as, apparently, it wasn't one of their own that made it. That's okay, we never did it for them anyway. We never belonged, we never did, and for most of us, we never will, to either this country or our own people. We are a lost generation. We are first generation kids born in another country. We came here at an early age with really traditional parents desperately trying to hold on to what they knew. We were expected to fit into both the old and new ways, struggling at both, and it seems, for some of us, forever trying to find our way. We were and still are Hmong outlaws. This was our way of finally belonging to something special. And we did it because we were all in on what we believed. Ladies and gentlemen, I ask you to believe again.

If there's one thing you should take from this section, it's that belief is the most important thing to success – that is why I spent so much time talking about it. Belief is how you can come from the refugee camps to make it in America. Belief is how you can make it to the State

Championships. Belief is how you can go from the worst sales reps in the history of mankind to one of the best. Belief is the only way you can be All In. When you believe in yourself, when you truly become, then you don't need to dodge the bullets of life anymore. You can just stop them in mid-air, like Neo at the end of the movie, when he finally believed and became The One.

Chapter 11 #Truths

- Rule #1: Always look good
- If you can't find a hero, be your own hero
- They can laugh all they want, they can't stop you, only you can stop you
- Success is the best revenge
- Believe in yourself and you can make history

Step 2: Own the #Truth

"With Great Power Comes Great Responsibility."

-Spiderman

Chapter 12: Own the #Truth

Before you can begin anything worthwhile in life, you must own the #truth. What does that mean exactly? It means taking 200% responsibility. You must take 100% responsibility for all the things you did and 100% of all the things you didn't do in life to be where you are at today - together 200%. This is probably the hardest step to do. Most people will go through life never owning it, never taking responsibility for anything. They will blame everyone and everything for all the things that didn't turn out exactly how they imagined it. They go around listening to the haters, the noise, the lies, the opinions, the negativity, and the people who don't know anything about what's really important to them. They're so busy that they never get a chance to focus and work on themselves, find out who they truly are, and what's really important to them. This is what holds people back the most and it is the one of the most important things you can ever do for yourself.

Most people can own up to all the positive things that they've done, but very few will ever own up to the negative things and the #truth, whether it was their direct fault or not. With the successes, they go around saying, "I did all myself! I never had anyone help me! It was all me!" With the failures in their life, they go around saying, "It was this guy's fault or that guy's fault! My parents were poor, I didn't' have any family help, my dad's a drunk, my teachers were idiots, my bosses were mean, my wife or husband doesn't do anything so I divorced them! If I didn't have this problem or that tragedy, I'd be great right now!" It's natural to do so, that's just how we're built. It's a defense mechanism so that we're able to deal with the rigors of life. However, it's not the whole truth and you must break free from this cycle. It will allow gratefulness to come into your life and it will free you to learn from everyone, not just the people you admire. Everyone can be a teacher or a mentor, not just successful, rich, powerful people. You can take lessons from even the worst people – if anything, it's what not to do.

Even after I failed massively in business and had every logical reason to blame everyone and everything, the truth was that nobody put a gun to my head to join the business, to make the decisions I made, and I didn't succeed because who I was just wasn't enough to succeed. Anything else is just not taking full responsibility. Without owning up to this, I could never have moved on to find my true calling in life. I'd still be stuck in the woods somewhere, hacking away in frustration and misery. Without owning up to this, I would still be focusing on the past, focusing on things that don't matter, and on people that don't matter anymore to my life. That's why I choose not to focus on my failed business and all the things my partner did, I only choose to focus on the lessons I've learned. If anything, what you focus on will persist and grow, so by focusing on the past, on unimportant things, and on other people, that's what you'll end up getting. This could only take away from what you need to do and who you want to be. Time is so precious to waste and you never know how long you have, so you must own up to who you are right now and make a powerful decision to be who you want to be. At the end of the day, who you want to be and becoming that person is all that matters. Now you just have to go out and bridge the gap between who you are right now and who you want to be.

You always knew and you have always known that every time you have failed at something in your life - on a test, your grades, in college, your job or job promotion, your marriage, raising your kids, your health and fitness, business, or your sales budget - it was because you didn't put in the work and you didn't do what was required of you to get the job done. Period. You would much rather procrastinate, take the easy way out, focus on the weeds and the negativity, watch TV, play video games, watch

Football, hang out with the boys, play on your phone, eat, sleep, not deal with it, blame the economy, blame the weather, blame others, not face your fears, not work as hard, not fight for it, play the victim, say that it was too hard, say that it was going to take too much money, say you just don't know enough, say that you're just not ready yet, not do whatever it takes, or any number of perfectly great reasons. But honestly, take a deep look at all your failures in life, if you would have believed in yourself more, if you wanted it bad enough, if you would have stuck it through, had the discipline, taken the time, put in the effort, put in the money, taken a chance, and didn't quit, you know would have succeeded. That's why most people only regret the things they don't do in life, not all the things they actually did – whether it ended in success or in failure.

I could have easily said that my parents' ended up in America too late, that I started school too late, that they were poor and so were all my relatives, that I was bullied and ridiculed growing up, so I should just give up on any delusions of grandeur. If I said that to myself and allowed that excuse to exist in my reality, there would have been no way I would become valedictorian, especially when I first told people and they all just laughed at me. I didn't listen to them and I never let doubt cross my mind. I guarantee that if I did, especially when it was really tough during the fifth and sixth grades, I would have quit. I was still in ESL (English as a Second Language) class along with all my similar age cousins and friends. They were having a grand ole time just speaking to each other in Hmong while I was trying to get rid of my accent and convince the teachers that I was ready for the big time – regular reading and writing classes. No more of the daily "stove" "window" "car" word association games during ESL classes. My cousins felt slighted for some reason, "What? You think you're better than us?" I'm just determined to prove everyone wrong about us and since it's not going to be you guys, it might as well be me. My uncles and aunts thought my parents tried to set me up to fail. They'd tell me things like, "Oh

Bolo, you're Hmong, we don't do things like this, we have to be respectful and humble" or "Come on, Bolo, we're Hmong, we'll never be as good as white people, this is their language, we're in their country." They'd tell their kids not to hang out with me for fear that my attitude might rub off on them. I could have been more Hmong-like or more modest, but I didn't have any room for such thoughts, so I told them to watch as I'm going to show them. I've got no time for fears, no time for doubts, and no room for excuses, especially because I was so far back already. The only thoughts in my head were dreams of conquest and thoughts of victory, and nobody was going to get in my way of my success. I was All In.

My parents put me in summer school all the way until we got to high school. We never went on family vacations like most people did. When everyone came back to school the teachers would ask them what they did on their summer break and the kids would tell the most amazing stories. Mine was always the same - my brother and I stayed home, went to summer school to catch up, and read a lot of books at the Willows Public Library where my mom worked. In retrospect, even though I felt some resentment at the time toward my parents for not having money for family vacations and putting my brother and I in summer school every year while my cousins played around all summer, those were the most formative years of my life and allowed me to catch up to all the other kids and eventually surpass them. While most of the kids came back from vacation and forgot most things they learned the year before, I was catching up. While most kids took several months to catch up on all they forgot, I was getting better every day and getting ahead. All of a sudden, these people that were seemingly untouchable once a upon a time started becoming my competition. After the eighth grade, I knew it was only a matter of time. I was selected to give a graduation speech for the eighth grade graduates, and that was when all my uncles and aunts saw me shine and started to believe that I was serious all along. That was when they started letting my cousins hang out with my brother and I hoping something would rub off on them.

It was a great lesson in human nature. I learned that people want you to succeed and generally want what's best for you, but just not better than them. When I was an upstart they laughed at me, ridiculed me, put me down, or at best, patronized me so I would stay beneath them or just like them at best. Like most people, they seem to always know what's best for me and exactly what I should or shouldn't be doing. But the #truth is that, like most people, they usually don't have a damn clue what they should be doing themselves so all they do is hate. They tried their best to hate on me when I started doing well. When I started doing better than them, they tried to tear me down, bully me, rat on me, team up on me, distance themselves from me, and put me in time-out.

I remember one day in the 8th grade, I was waiting in line for lunch when a white boy, whom I still remember to this day, cut right in front of me. That particular day, I didn't eat breakfast and remembered being really hungry. All the kids started complaining and yelling for the yard-duty to come make things right. When she came over to inquire about the commotion, all the kids pointed to the boy saying that he had cut in line, but he instead lied and said I was in fact the one that had cut in line. Bewildered, I turned to the kids for help, but it was to no avail because she immediately, forcibly, and assuredly yanked me out of line, despite the protests of all the other kids. I was tossed in time-out in tears, shock, and disbelief. I've never been in time-out before! When the time-out was over, I went back the end of the line, but lunch was already over and I was devastated. By that time, I wasn't even hungry anymore anyway. Those two hours after lunch were the longest hours I ever had to suffer through as I just sat quietly in class trying not to cry. After school when my dad came to pick my brother and I up from school, I just quickly got in and slammed the car door shut bursting into tears. I cried all the way home while my dad tried to calm me down and understand what had transpired. After several hours, I was finally able to explain what happened and he made a phone call to the principal to have a meeting. The next day my father and I met in the principal's office to discuss the situation. The principal simply said he was sorry for the "misunderstanding". Unfortunately, the damage had already been done. The pathetic apology was a slap in the face, and the betrayal was already complete to this kid. This single personal traumatic experience would serve as a reminder of the fear and injustice present in this town that would leave a scar on me for years to come. It was also a great lesson in human nature and drove me to do whatever it took to succeed as the best form of revenge and protection. I promised myself I was never going to let anyone tear me down again. The next time someone tries to tear me down, I will stand up for myself.

Soon, they'll say it was because I was lucky, or smart, or had an advantage over them. Then when I can't be ignored anymore, they'll want their kids to be more like me. Very few people can see the success of other people and root for them to do better than them. Successful people are the only ones who don't hate on the success of other successful people. It's because they have been through it themselves and know how hard it was, how much struggle there must have been, how much fear and courage was involved in the process, and how much overcoming had to be done to get where they got. One of my successful contractor friends used to tell me all the time, "If I knew how hard it was going to be going in, I would never have done it." They've been there and they've walked in the shoes.

The interconnected path of fear, blame, and victimization was so pervasive when I was growing up in the refugee camp and it remains the same here. I've seen it since I was just a little boy in Chieng Kham Refugee Camp in Thailand. I had always seen it, felt it, heard about it, and knew it existed even when I couldn't understand it. Ask almost any Hmong person old enough to remember, and most will tell you that they hate Thai people.

The only safe haven was in Thailand after the war. Laos belonged to the communists after the U.S. pulled out so the next closest refuge was in Thailand. The U.N. had set up refugee camps near the border just inside Thailand after you cross the Mekong River, which was the border separating Laos and Thailand. We can't be allowed to escape and mix with the general population. Obviously, these barb-wire surrounded camps, which held thousands of uncivilized, barbaric people had to be guarded by Thai people. These were the only Thai people that we ever really came into contact with. Pretty much all of them were corrupt as they come and most of us feared and hated them. The 20 or so Thai guards and their families would take half the rations dropped from helicopters and divide the rest among the thousand of refugees they were guarding. Then they would use that as bargaining chips. The elders quickly and most especially hated them. The adults hated them or kissed their asses, one or the other. The kids feared and hated them as well, mostly taught by their parents and grandparents to do so – all the way to America.

I remember one fine day my cousins and I were playing next to the Thai guard station – it was really only the flattest ground to play on. It was always a risk-reward situation depending on the mood of the guards. We were throwing rocks as kids like to do. A rock ricocheted and landed near their door where they were drunk or bored or both. They came running after us and we all took off. My cousin Tong was too slow so they were able to grab him while the rest of us escaped. This time it was severe. They threw him in jail for 3 days and took turns kicking the shit out of him…literally. To this day, we make fun of him and tell him we'll beat the shit out of him. His dad had to go beg the guards to let him go. They made his dad crawl under their legs – for those who don't know, this is the worst shame for a grown Asian man. This act represented being lower than a dog. You would have to kill most men before they would do such a thing. It's the equivalent of giving up all your manhood. Revenge and murder had been committed for even suggesting that certain men did such an act. But for his oldest boy, my uncle had to do it. My uncle still obviously hates Thais more than anyone you'll ever meet. He often promises to kill every single living Thai on this planet if given the chance. These were some of the experiences we had growing up in the refugee camps. And this was only from the untrained young child's eye. God only knows what the adults and elders saw and experienced.

It was only when I came down to Long Beach from Northern California and met some Thai people at restaurants and school that changed my mind. Much to my dismay, they weren't just nice Thai people, they were some of the nicest people I had ever met, ever. That questioned my whole perspective on Thai people. The questions kept burning in the back of my mind for years until I started working for The Paint Company right out of college. Back then, if upper management wanted to get rid of you, they'd "promote" you to the outskirts of the region, which was normally Oxnard up north, Cathedral City in the Inland Empire to the east, or Temecula down south. These employees lived in the Los Angeles area so they would have to commute over 2 hours each way to work and they had almost zero support from management so inevitably they would quit sooner or later. It was much easier to do that than to fire them and suffer some sort of backlash like massive paperwork or wrongful termination lawsuits. That's when I realized why we got the worst of the worst Thai people in the world guarding us. Think about it, if you were a lieutenant or captain of the army and you had to send your people to the middle of nowhere, the jungle, to guard a bunch of uncivilized tribes, would you send your friends or people you don't like? The answer was, is, and always will be obvious. Most people would do the same. Growing up, my elders would tell stories of how terrible Thai people were. They tried to teach me to hate Thais, but my parents would always say, "Take a look at your own people, we're not exactly all angels ourselves. Son, every race has bad eggs and good eggs." I had a choice to make. Was I going to let my own experiences determine my destiny or was I going to decide my own fate? I chose to not hate Thai people anymore. I made friends with Kit and his sister, Angela, the owners of my favorite restaurant, Thai BBQ, in Long Beach. They were some of the nicest people I've ever met. Unfortunately, Kit passed away shortly and I never got the chance to thank him. I will never be late again in telling people I love them, I'm sorry, or I forgive them.

Blame makes you focus on the wrong things. When you focus on the wrong things, you don't do much of the right things that you should be doing. You will keep chasing the wrong things and the wrong people all your life until you take responsibility for who you really are and what you really want. When you stop blaming everyone and everything, when you stop lying to yourself, when you stop playing the victim, when you give up the BS stories you've been telling yourself all your life, when you see things for what they were - the past - that is when you will be free to pursue the life you were meant to live. If you are constantly toiling in the past, you'll never make the time to work on what you need to work on in the present. For some, including me, sometimes you are your own worst enemy. For whatever reason, usually through no fault of your own or when you were too young and ignorant to prevent it, you have it in your head that you don't deserve to receive love, money, success, gratitude, or happiness. Knock it off. You deserve it! You are not God, stop being so high and mighty and punishing yourself all the time. For now, get out of your own way so you can be successful. You're going to need it because it's going to take everything you have and more to achieve your goals and dreams. If you're constantly being bogged down by unimportant things like lies, blame, and the past, you won't take the necessary responsibility you need right now to succeed. Without taking responsibility, you're just not going to focus on what's important in your life. Without knowing what's important, you'll have little to no gratitude. Without gratitude you will never be happy.

I had to own up to the fact that I used to be the most grateful person on earth – coming from the lowest station in life and rising to achieve the American Dream, then failing massively by my own actions, becoming miserable, and contemplating suicide – but I became an ungrateful person who didn't see that he had the world in his hands already.

So you must stop blaming your problems, your reasons, your excuses, your unfair sales budget, your circumstances, your parents, your family, your wife, your bosses, your friends, or anyone else and anything else as to why you're not getting the results you're looking for. Your boss is an asshole, so what, he's not going make you successful. You have to own the #truth about your success or lack there-of. You must stop waiting for somebody else to change your life for you. Like I said earlier, nobody will do your pushups for you. The only way you will get the results you want is to take full 200% responsibility for your life, all of it, even the bad stuff, even if it was not due to your direct and conscious decision-making. It could have been your parent's fault that you ended up in the situation that you did, but now that you're reading this, you have the power to change your future forever, starting right now.

Chapter 12 #Truths

- Own the #Truth
- Take responsibility for the good and the bad, direct or indirect
- Stop the blame
- Live in the present moment
- Stop Focusing on the past
- Own up to who you really are right now
- Decide who you want to be, then go bridge the gap between who you are right now and who you want to be
- Every time you failed, it was just because you didn't put in enough
- People always know about what you need to do, but have no clue what they need to do
- It's easier to tear someone down than to build one's self up
- Successful people don't hate on other people's successes like the unsuccessful
- There are bad eggs in every batch
- Focus on the right things, let go of the wrong things

Chapter 13: Time and Money

There is a difference between knowing and believing. You know with your brain, but you believe with your heart. If there's one lesson that I've learned above all else about my time here on earth and about human nature, it's that when you know, you may not necessarily do it, but when you believe, you will do whatever it takes. Just like getting fit, pretty much everyone inherently knows what it takes to be fit. In fact, it's actually quite simple. It's called…wait for it…diet and exercise. Mind-blowing, right? But not many people do it though. They don't do it because they don't believe in what they want enough. They always find excuses as to why they can't do it. They tried, they'll tell you. No time and no money are the two most overused and abused excuses in the world today.

"I would be fit too if I didn't have a real 9-5 job and have to take care of my family" is probably the most common excuse used by modern people who are unsuccessful at being fit or any other endeavor they've always wanted to pursue.

"I need my 8-10 hours of sleep" is also a good one, similar to "I'm not a morning person."

"I don't know anything about this subject and I just don't know anyone who I can turn to for help" is also very prevalent for those wishing to use ignorance as an excuse.

"I don't have the money" is a classic!

There are literally an infinite amount of excuses or what they call it, "reasons" that people can and do use to avoid the real truth that they are just lying to themselves so they don't feel bad. It's just much easier to tear others down, to blame others, to blame your circumstances, to avoid the #truth, give into your fears, avoid owning up to your responsibilities, and avoid keeping your promise to yourself than to do what is hard and own the fact that you just didn't do whatever it took, you weren't all in. When you are All In, you will find a way no matter the odds stacked against you.

"Sure, it makes sense, you have a regular 9-5 day job, you have a wife or husband, you have kids, you have family and friends, it makes sense and is okay to let yourself go, get fat, I mean, who has time for the gym? Being fit is only for actors or actresses that are paid to look good. It's only for douche-bags at the gym because of course it makes sense that they have no jobs so they have all day to work out and look at themselves in the mirror. It makes sense. You're tired. You're stressed from work. You've got projects that you need to complete around the house. You need your sleep. You have to watch your favorite TV shows. You've got all these things planned. You have to keep up with the Joneses. Nobody would blame you. You're doing what normal, reasonable logical people do. Who has time anymore? This is just who you are." Sound familiar?

Most people know what they need to do to fix any situation in their lives, they are not idiots, but they don't believe in it enough to do what it takes. They know what it will take to fix their marriage, but they don't. They know what it takes to raise great kids, but they don't. They know they need to stop smoking, drinking, and any other bad habit, but they don't. They know how to lose weight. But they just don't want it bad enough. They know what it takes to be a great freaking salesman, but they don't. This applies to most things in life. They know in their heads, but they don't believe in their hearts. When you don't believe, then you won't be able to own up to what's really going on with you. You'll say one thing but do another. You'll say what makes sense but you don't actually do it. You'll recite normal, reasonable, logical rhetoric that every normal, reasonable, logical person says just because it sounds good and makes sense as to why you're not successful yet. The fact is, if you actually believe in what you're saying, you will just do it.

For a while there, I was a perpetually horrendous sales rep in my early years. Then came the point at which I had had enough of sucking. At that point, I might've been fine if I was even just mediocre at my job but I couldn't even manage that. I had to take a mini vacation by myself to Palm Springs to do nothing but put pen to paper on how much I sucked, why I sucked, what worked, what didn't, what I wasn't doing, what I know I should be doing, enough of the "My boss is an asshole and I didn't get any training so that's why I suck, just wait till I have a new better boss" excuses, the timewasters and real activities that produced the best results, and really just owned up the #truth about where I was at. No BS. Shoot, aside from jotting down reminders and notes, I hadn't even touched a pen in the 10 years since graduating college. In that condensed weekend, I went through all the stages of change that any human being has to go through when dealing with change: Denial, Struggle, Exploration, and All-In. Denial is an obvious one, I could not believe that I never sold a day in my life even though it's been two years since I became a rep! It took a while for that to really sink in. That was probably the hardest part. Then I was pretty sad as I struggled to grasp how much I sucked at sales. For Goodness Sake, I was nothing but a glorified order taker! All I did was go from shop to shop asking if my contractors had any jobs for me or just waited for the phone to ring so they could give me orders and then just do my very best not to screw up the order. It was not fun. In fact, it's down-right excruciating to think so lowly and honestly of myself. I would have chopped off my left pinky than to go through that. That's why most reps will never be able to do that. Some things like humility and change are just too beneath them. They just know everything already. Their cups way too filleth over. That is why they will be perpetually mediocre their whole entire sales careers. I've known many a rep who have all the natural sales talents and charisma but are always at $1.5 Million in sales, flat, year after year after year for decades – adjusted for inflation, they're actually getting worse every year.

After much struggle, I started taking notes and exploring how I can start becoming a great sales rep. I started to get out of The Shit, as I call it, and started focusing. From then on, I became a master at putting pen to paper which has helped me to crystalize any thoughts and beliefs I've had, get rid of the unimportant noise and BS inside my head, and focus all my efforts on what's most important. What was most apparent was that I never took any sales coaching or seminars aside from the mandatory one that my company originally sent me to as a rookie, which I'd already forgotten everything about anyway. Then I took inventory of what worked and what didn't. I measured all my activities and made a plan to focus on the ones that produced the most results and do less of the time wasters. I made a plan, I put it on a timeline made of multi-colored Post-It notes across my hotel room walls, then put it all on a schedule with an estimate of how much time and money I would have to invest in myself – and let me tell you, whatever I thought it was back then, it was way more time and money than I'd ever imagined. Sales coaches, sales seminars, sales training programs on audio-CD, books, magazines, DVD's, Youtube videos, and anything else I could get my hands on. The funny thing was that during the time of this writing, I've never once seen any sales rep from the painting industry come to one seminar. That's why I'm the best in my industry. I simply put in more time and money than anyone from my industry. Period. The last thing I did was become All In. I was going to develop whatever skills and habits needed to become the absolute best freaking sales rep I can possibly be. I was going to do whatever it takes. I was All In.

Ultimately though, just like with everything, the proof is in the doing; otherwise, it's just all talk. The proof, to me, is where you put in the time and the money. Those two things are generally two of the most important things to people so if you look at how they spend it, you'll objectively see who they really are, not what they say or how they feel about it, just what is. Owning it. Being All In. Take a real look at how people spend their time and their money, that is what's important to them, what they really want, and who they really are. Everything else is just BS. Everything else is just wishy-washy lies and excuses they tell themselves and others so they could feel good about themselves. So own the #truth.

BFF

I had a friend four years ago who was extremely obese and came to me for advice – we will call him BFF.

BFF asked me, "Bolo, I really wanna lose weight! What's your secret?"

"Secret? Ha! Ain't no secret, Man! It's just called diet and exercise, Bro!" I told him.

He replied, "There's no way it's that easy, Man!"

I told him it wasn't easy, but it's that simple. Everyone knows you just have to eat clean and exercise more, but nobody really does it. Why? They don't believe it. Since they don't believe it, their actions don't align with it and they don't get the results they want. It's like that with anything in life. Most people don't do what they know, they do what they believe. That's all that matters. Everything else, like I said, is BS. BFF pleaded to me that he's always been big-boned. He told me his family were all fat – his mom and dad and all his brothers and sisters - so he's destined to be fat. I mean, just look at the evidence right? Ever since he can remember he's been a fat boy. Ever since high school he's been pushing three bills. But he told me he really wanted to lose weight. He said he's always wanted to lose weight all his life but just doesn't know how. He begged me to tell him how. He proclaimed that he would do whatever it takes to be skinny. I said he needed to get a gym membership, first of all.

"How much is it?" he asked. I told him about $30 a month.

"$30 dollars! That's too expensive!"

I screamed back, "Really, BFF? Really? Ya see, that's why you're fat, Bro! A minute ago, you were begging me and telling me you would do whatever it takes, and now you're saying $30 is too much! Come on, Man! Here's the thing, if you really wanted something, money is no issue! You will pay whatever price it is if you really wanted it. If you can't afford, you will work for it, create the money for it, and save for it. Besides, if you actually sat down and looked at how much money you spend on getting fat, you will be amazed! If you actually calculate how much money you spend on fast foods, fatty foods, sugary foods and drinks, and general fat foods, I'm willing to bet it's close to around a thousand dollars a month, and you don't have $30 for a gym membership?!" He didn't know the half of it - healthy foods would probably cost more.

Ashamed, he said, "Well, okay, I guess you're right, but well, so then, how many times do I have to work out a week then?"

I said, every single day for an hour.

What? Wow, that's too much time, Man, I don't have that much time, he exclaimed.

I about lost it, "Oh my God, really? You said you really wanted it, but an hour a day is too much for you? Come on, Man! You gotta make the damn time! An hour a day is nothing! Have you ever calculated the time you make for getting fat? Let me tell you! I don't have to be a fly on your wall but I know exactly who you are because I've been there! You spend most of your time looking for fat places to eat and finding fat foods. Then you sit down somewhere comfortable to eat them, mostly your couch. Then you sit on your couch and do fat activities like napping, playing on your phone, watching all your favorite TV shows, playing video games, drinking sugary drinks, and eating chips! That's a lot of hours getting fat, Man! And not one hour was spent trying to be fit! So be honest, Man! You say you wanna be skinny, but who you are is a fat person, Bro! You spend most of your time and most of your money getting fat, not getting skinny! That's who you are. Those are your actions! That's why you're fat!"

The #truth finally hit him. Mouth opened, looking sad and dumbfounded, he fidgeted around while his eyes started to shimmer like tears were about to burst. I could see it in his eyes that he just realized he's been spending most of his time and money somewhere other than where he said he really wanted. He stopped lying to himself. He put away the bullshit, the excuses, the blame, and all those perfectly logical and reasonable reasons. He finally knew what's really important. He believed, then took a giant leap of faith and made a decision. That day he finally made a real decision to become fit. He decided to put his time and money where his mouth is. A year later, he dropped over 125 pounds. He went from 300 down to 175.

How did he do it? He wanted it bad enough, first of all. He was All In. Enough to cut the bullshit and excuses and did whatever it took. Ignorance was not an excuse. Time was not an excuse. Money was not an excuse. Neither was work, life, family, tired, sad, sore, hurt, hot, cold, dark, rain, pain, or any other excuses. He had to build up the muscles in his mind first before it would manifest itself physically. Like everything else in life. He had to do whatever it took to bridge the gap between being a fat person and who he wanted to be, a fit person. That meant he had to work on his mind and his actions every single day so that they align with who he wanted to be. All he would do was buy and do healthy stuff. He made the time to wake up every day at 4 A.M., drive to his gym an hour away in El Segundo, CA from his house in El Monte, and put in at least one hour of sweat equity and learn about nutrition. In fact, soon, an hour a day was not enough for him. He was doing twice-a-day's most of the time. He made the time to do research on people and things he didn't know. He would Google it, ask me and others questions about it, call and text his trainer daily about any questions including about alcohol consumption and what type and how much if he had to drink alcohol. He would buy healthy foods, took time to prep those healthy foods, and eat those healthy foods, and it got to the point where even when he's eating healthy food, he's thinking about his next healthy meal or meals already. He joined not one but two gyms. He did P90-X and Insanity. He went Paleo for a while. In fact, he tried almost every type of diet there was until he found the one diet that suited him and his lifestyle the best. He even did a little cross-fit. Cross-fit! A grown ass man! He even bought his own dumbbells and bench set and returned mine back to me. He joined workout groups. He was finally All In. He believed in it enough to put in the time and the money because it was truly important to him. He finally did what it took, All In, and trained his mind and his actions to be fit, and thus became fit.

Lyon

I had another friend who was a manager at one of my stores – we'll call him Lyon. Great guy, very well liked, team player, always willing to help others, can always be counted on to get anything done, especially when the bosses needed him to do something for the entire district, but never mentioned in the same breath as some of the young hotshots and rising stars that management was looking to promote. Lyon was much like The Typical Jose, and looked at the same way as well. Lyon was given projects and stuff that nobody else wanted to do because he would always stay longer – even off the clock – to get it done, with no incentives other than a pat on the back. It didn't even help his bottom line; in fact, it took from it, because of the running around he would have to do on top of his day to day job. He was the type of manager who knew everything; knew a lot of people, very dependable, never late, really nice, took the time to honestly and thoroughly answer anyone and everyone's questions, and if you were in a bind, you could call him up and he will do anything to get it done – in short, a godsend to any young upstart who is lucky enough to have known him and been trained underneath him. However, he was horrible for assistants and employees who were lazy and took advantage of it – and he had a few back to back. That meant that on top of all the projects and activities the bosses were throwing his way because they knew he would get it done no matter what, he would be doing everything at his store as well while his assistants sat on their asses and feigned ignorance. He's the type of guy who relishes hard work, and as he says, "I'm Mexican, that's what we do! I pride myself on hard work!"

I'd say, "Come on, Bro! I'm Hmong, that's all we know too, but ya gotta learn to work smarter! I'm not in Thailand anymore and you're not in freakin' Mexico anymore! I did the same thing as a manager for years and where did it get me? All my other buddies got promoted so much faster than me, making so much more money than me now, and they never even mixed a gallon of paint while I worked my ass off, literally bled for this freakin' company, and almost died several times. They'd tell me, "I'm a manager! I don't mix paint! That's what I got Mexicans for!" They had a plan, they built the right relationships, and they delegated expertly while I worked my ass off! 60-70 hours a week average for several years and all I got was getting passed over numerous times. I tried to do everything, just like you. So I sucked just like you, just like most good managers and reps. Most good managers and reps focus on everything else but the most important things. Those who try to do everything never succeed at anything. They just clap while others walk. They put out fires, they take every call, mix every gallon of paint, reply to all the emails, do all the work, help all the customers, and try to do everything themselves while the subordinates under them just get complacent – it actually does the opposite and stalls their development. All for what? Managers do not manage things, they manage people, that's why it's called Management and not Doing Things. You must learn to manage and not just do everything!"

He didn't listen to me until his store started suffering. This was his second store he was managing. The first was in Riverside, CA where he was over-worked, underpaid, carrying the whole store, and why he wanted out in the first place. On top of that, he was having to drive about 2 hours each way to work. He was going to quit so management found my old store, near his house and family, in Huntington Beach for him to manage. It was supposed to be his new start and the beginning of something great – a second chance and more family time. But as we all know, if you don't change who you are, you will get the same usual results. A change of scenery will not change who you are unless you change your actions. As the saying goes, you can take the boy out of the hood, but you can't take the hood out of the boy, or in my case, the jungle.

He came to me in tears one day at the office when I was visiting him. He said he couldn't take it anymore. I said, "I agree, I couldn't take it for you a year ago when I saw you going through the same thing you were going through in Timbuktu Riverside. I tried to warn you, Bro, but you didn't listen. I told you a year ago to be careful, because you were going down the same exact path I was going before I came to this store. Now you even have your damn wife delivering paint for you, too? Are you freakin' crazy? What happens if she gets in an accident doing your work for you? Instead of the company commending you for working like a true freakin' Mexican, instead of the company being amazed at your dedication – they would fire your ass in a heart-beat because of the liability and PR storm! You're right, Man, you're just dumbass! You've got a large family you have to take care of! What were you thinkin'? Jeez, Lyon, I love you but this is all your damn fault, Bro! At the end of the day, what's important, huh? Your bosses, who don't give a crap about you and take advantage of you? Or your lazy ass assistants, who just sit back and watch you do everything because you want to anyway? Or you, taking advantage of finally being given a second chance to be a real manager as opposed to being a highly paid glorified Mexican full time paint mixer? Or are you going to do what your dad, God Bless his soul, wanted you to be and be more than how you were born? He would want you to be smart, take care of your large family because he's gone, and take care of number one! You guys were dirt poor all your lives, you told me many times, living in cars, no electricity, hungry all the time, even when you were growing up here in America, and now that you're given the opportunity to be more than poor, to never be poor again, and you don't do anything different! Your dad is turning over in his grave right now, Man!"

Tears started rolling down his face at the #truth. He said, "Oh my god, Bolo, you're right. From now on, I'm going to look out for number one. I'm going to look out for my family. I'm going to be more than a dumbass…but how? How do I finally become a real manager?"

I said, "First, you need to pick up Stephen Covey's book called, The 7 Habits of Highly Effective People."

Lyon then asked, "Well how much is that?"

Surprised, I said, "It's like fifteen bucks."

"What? That's too much money!" he gasped.

Irate, I screamed, "Really? Jeez Luis, Lyon! I give up! You deserve to be poor, Man! For god sakes, you're eating a $12 fast food meal from McDonald's for lunch right now! And you don't have $15 for the most fundamental book there is to management? And you say you want to be a manager? Come on, Man! I'm done! I'm done!"

Realizing his own stupidity, he said, "Um…uh…I guess you're right, well, what is the book about anyways?"

I told him, "It's about how to be an effective person, Man, as the title says! It's only the most basic and popular book about how to be a good manager and whatever else you wanna apply it to! It's the book that changed my life forever when I was a hard-working, getting-nowhere manager like yourself to who I am now! I was there just like you and this book changed everything! It started me on the basic fundamentals that poor Mexicans like yourself and poor little Mongols like me never got from our people and our society where we came from! Fifteen bucks is nothing, Bro! Ya see, fifteen bucks is nothing when you want something bad enough! For god sakes, you're already eating a $12 Super-Sized meal that doesn't do nothin' for you but clog up your arteries! And you don't even need to eat for 27 days and you'll still be alive! And you can't cough up another three bucks for this book? If you add up all your Super-Sized meals that you eat every single day, it would be over $300 a month and you're tellin' me you can't afford fifteen bucks to invest in your family so they can be not so poor and have a chance at being well off later on? Come on, Man! Are you that stupid? That's the proof right there man! The reason why you're poor and fat is because you spend money like poor people and fat people do! You don't invest in yourself and your family at all, fifteen bucks is even too much for you, but you would spend countless money on being poor and fat! All your money is spent on being poor and fat. All your time is spent on being poor and fat. You never buy books or invest in yourself. You never spent a minute reading or investing in yourself, or asking people and learning from people who have something to teach you about being successful and smart. I know this well because I was you! You work, work, work, then go home and watch all your favorite TV shows, you never miss an episode, follow every single stat from every player on every single one of your favorite teams, you buy and play all the newest games and video game systems that come out – which if you think about it, is like $60 dollars a game, and the system itself is over $500 – so you can waste time, play sports, drink beer, hang out with friends and family all day long, but you don't have fifteen bucks to invest in yourself, invest in your family, invest in knowledge, invest in wisdom, and invest in your future! Come on, Man! Time and Money! Honestly, where do you spend it? Because right now, fifteen bucks is too much for you to spend where it actually counts, and all you're doing is lying to yourself, crying for no reason to me like a little bitch that you really want to change your situation, but all you want is for me to lie to you like everyone else does, to pat you on your stupid back, and feed you lies that you already tell yourself every day so you can sleep better! You don't want this! Be honest! You don't want to be a good manager! Your actions prove otherwise! Your actions are the opposite! What do you want, Lyon?"

Flabbergasted at the #truth, he sighed, "I want to not be poor and stupid anymore..."

"Good, then go get that book, right now" I said.

Then how fast did the lies come back as he said, "Well, I don't even know where to get it. I mean, I don't have money right now because I just bought and ate my lunch with it. And I gotta get back to work anyway."

Absolutely floored, I yelled, "Oh my freakin' God, Lyon! I'm done, I'm freakin' done! You came to me freakin' crying, Dude! Really? I hate to be so mean to you like this, but I have to! Nobody else will! This is what a real friend does, not those people who talk smack behind your back and pretend to be nice in front of you. I have to be brutally honest with you, Bro, because that's the only way you're gonna listen, but seriously, you're really pissin' me off now! Thanks for wasting my time. Don't have money? Again? You can't take out a freakin' credit card? You're already in debt, you were just done telling me that! Another fifteen dollars at Barnes and Nobles right down the street is not going to make you anymore broke than you already are! If anything, if anything, if you want it bad enough, it would only help you and help your family who you don't deserve right now! You don't have time? You just got done crying to me, listening to me slap you around for half an hour, wasting my time, stuffing your face with your Big Mac, and you don't have fifteen minutes to run down to the Barnes and Nobles on the same street we're on, go to the self-help or business section, and get this fifteen dollar book? I give up, Man, you are going to be a poor and stupid for the rest of your life!"

Ashamed, he said, "Okay, Bolo, okay, you're right, I promise I'll do what you say go to Barnes and Nobles! But I'll go after work, I promise I'll do what you say. You're right."

Shaking my head, I said, "No, Lyon, you still don't get it. If I said that this book was a million dollars in cash waiting for you to trade in $15, would you do it, would you go get it right now? Because it could! Who knows, nobody knows, but it could open up Pandora's Box for you and allow you to access more than millions, maybe billions, who knows! But you've got your head so far up your ass that you still don't get it. I don't need you to do what I say. I don't care about you doing what I want. I don't need nothin' from you but for you to do what YOU say you will do and take care of your family. Don't do it for me, Amigo. Do it for you! Do what you say you will do for YOU! Do what you say for your family! Do what you say for your people! Do what you say for your legacy! You don't get it, Lyon! Let me tell your future for you, please listen carefully.

You will NOT get the book after work, I promise you. You will do what you know and run around being poor. Some things will come up as they usually do, like your emails, your HR issues, your boss, your customers, your wife, your kids, your problems, then you'll forget about this book. Then you'll go home and do the same poor things you normally do. Another week will go by and I'll come visit you like I do every week and ask if you've gotten the book like you say you truly want to during our conversation today, and you'll tell me that you got busy and some problems came up so you couldn't. Then you'll promise me you'll get it soon. Then another week will come by, and I'll ask you again, and you'll start to get defensive. Then another week will go by, and when I come back to visit during my normal time and you'll make an excuse to go take care of another urgent problem conveniently around this time, I'll ask your employees where you are, and they'll tell me that you told them you had to go take care of a customer and don't know what time you'll return. Then I will stop asking knowing human nature and what I used to do myself. Then time will go by, six months perhaps, everything will go according to what usually happens when nothing else changes – your work will suffer more, you'll get written up since it was only a matter of time, you'll get depressed again – same as usual. Then when you're about to get fired, then we'll have another conversation maybe, if you have enough balls to face me again, and I hope you do because I will always care for you more than you do yourself right now, and when you are ready, then we can have another conversation. Then you'll probably pick up the book, then it will take you another six months to read it, if ever, then when you've got no choice but to be fired and you are absolutely going to lose everything, then maybe you'll read the book and maybe your life will finally start to have intention, direction, and focus. Maybe then you'll come back and thank me, and I will tell you, don't thank me, Brother, thank yourself! I love you, Bro, remember that."

That's exactly how it happened by the way. I hate it when I'm right. I hate it when people say I'm good at telling the future. No, I'm not good at telling the future, I'm good at telling about human nature. I've just been there so many times and I'm just really good at understanding fear, failure, blame, excuses, human nature, and the #truth. I wish I wasn't good, but I am, because I paid for it with time and suffering…lots and lots of it. I don't wish that upon my worst enemy. And I certainly don't wish it for you.

Gordon

Gordon was a sales representative. He was the typical sales rep like myself a long time ago. He had everything it took to be a great sales rep, like most reps, that's why they're reps – because somebody saw that they were likeable, could communicate well, and had ambition. Like most reps though, he was floundering at the bottom of the pack for a while, like I was during my first two years as a new rep. Most reps take a year or two to be effective, if ever. It normally takes this long to figure out what not to do before they figure out what to do and their style of selling. He couldn't figure out why he just couldn't get the results the company was asking for, couldn't even hit budget, year after year. He came to me crying and depressed after being put on a 6-month probation review, and said he was tired of being mediocre. He asked me to teach him. He said he didn't know how to be a good sales rep and he wanted to know my secret.

I told him, "Bro, it's not a secret. It's never a secret. You know what it takes to be a good sales rep. You have what it takes to be a good sales rep. Everyone knows what they must do in life to be good at anything. You just have to apply my 4 Simple Steps to Success to achieve your wildest dreams! Most things are not rocket science, Man. Most things, like being a good business man, sales rep, husband, wife, parent, son, daughter, student, being fit, speaker, or whatever it may be – you already know how – but you don't believe so you don't do it. Here's an example: most people already know what the truth is when they hear or read a good quote such as, there is nothing to fear but fear itself. Everyone nods their head in agreement, maybe even try to save it for a rainy day, but then they just quickly move on and never take the time and effort to work on their fears, running away every single time fear comes up in their lives.

From the way you are looking at me, you still don't believe me. Again, let me say it slowly, you already know everything and you already have all it takes to be successful. "Oh but it's hard." No it's not hard. It's only hard because you don't believe so you really don't want it bad enough. "Oh it's too much money." Again you just don't want it bad enough. "Oh it's going to take too long." Again, you don't want it bad enough. My brother wanted to have his Ph.D. He didn't care that it took him 10 years of schooling and hundreds of thousands of dollars. I know guys who make less than me but own a Porsche or Corvette because they love cars and is All In on getting their car no matter what. And when you're All In, almost like magic, you always end up finding the time and the money to get what you want. Seriously, it's laughable sometimes. I have part-time drivers who can barely keep their jobs, still live at home, don't have time and money for anything, but they always somehow have the newest, shiniest, most custom rims on their cars. For cryin' out loud, it's worth more than their cars, Man! Same thing for guys who find time and money for the clubs, Vegas trips, fishing, hunting, guns, toys, sports, or whatever things they love. Time and money are no issues for them! Admittedly, I always find time and money for golf!

Look, Man, being a good sales rep is really simple – you already know! You just have to make a bunch of consistent telephone calls to fill your funnel, go see a bunch of people to build relationships and properly service them, then make a bunch of follow-up calls to make sure the customers are happy, if they got any more business coming up, and to keep building relationships. Like I said, it's not rocket science, Man!"

"It's not that simple, Bolo."

"Yes, it is. When you boil it down to the nitty-gritty, at its core, it's simple. It may not be easy, but it's simple. We are the ones who make it all complicated. We know it's simple, but we don't believe it. Just like in golf and just like in life.

My buddy, Jerry Maras, god bless his soul, may he finally rest in peace, the best golfer I've ever known in my life – taught me everything I know about golf, how to prepare, how to practice, doing what you love, and so much more about life - used to tell me all the time, "Cali, golf like life, is played within the six inches between your ears! First, you gotta focus on what you want! Don't focus on what you don't want! Don't focus on fear! Don't focus on where you don't want the ball to go, because you'll go there! Your mind can't tell the difference if it's good for you or not, it will only do what you focus on! You gotta focus on an exact spot! Visualize and see an exact spot where you want the ball to land in the fairway or on the green. Then hit right to it using the straightest line possible! The quickest path from point A to point B is a straight line, Cali! But most people take their club back all over the place, then swing back all over the place, and it's only by pure luck, pure chance that they ever hit it straight – and then they wonder "Where'd it go?" or "Why didn't it go straight?" or "What am I doing wrong?" If they actually manage to hit it straight, they won't be able to do it again. They can never string together a series of straight shots. That's why they're all over the place like their golf balls. Pew right. Then pew left. Then chunk. Then skull. Then in the woods. Penalty. Then in the bunker. Penalty. Then in the water. Penalty. Then they wonder why they can't break 100 at golf or in life or in sales!"

It all starts with believing. Because when you believe, your actions will show up and align with your words and your thoughts. With a plan, and focus, you'll be able to string together straight shots, wins, and get the results you want in life. It's that simple.

"See, I know because I've been there. I knew what it took, but without focus, like Jerry Maras would always tell me, without a definite goal or purpose, you can't focus on anything and you really don't know where you're going."

Jerry would always say, "Focus on your own game, Cali! Block out the distractions, Cali! Block out what everyone else is doing! Focus, focus, focus, you've got to focus, Cali!"

If you don't know where you're going, how can you possibly have a plan? Without a plan, you're all over the place. Outta sight, outta mind! Just like your sales results! You are never prepared. You look like a freakin' amateur, Man. It'll take you twice as long if you're lucky. Just fumbling around aimlessly, and only by pure luck, by pure chance that you get the results you're looking for – and you'll never be able to repeat it.

Like those guys who have a great year of sales because a big job landed in their laps. Then next year they tank. It's called Roller Coaster Reps! Up and down, up and down! I've seen it time and time again. Then when the crap hits the fan, they give up. Really nice guys, has everything it takes, but can never hit any budgets – always having an excuse like the economy, bad stores, customer issues, too much rain, some other problem why they can't hit their numbers – much less obliterate their budgets.

See, I've excelled at mediocre. Until I focused on what my purpose was. And no, my purpose in life is not slangin' paint, Bro. It's my family and it's a stepping stone to my ultimate mission in life – which is making a difference. You're already suffering, Bro. You're already an expert at being mediocre like I was. Until you believe, until you stop blaming and take responsibility, until you make a decision, and until you have the conviction to be excellent, you will always be mediocre. And it really doesn't take all that much to change.

You already have what it takes. You know it, I know it. I'm just pointing out the #truth to you. You just don't know how. But that's actually the easy part. You just have to change a couple of things. All it takes is just a little bit more than what you're doing right now. You don't have to demolish your whole life, revamp your whole plan, and bust everything up to high heaven. For example, some people already have everything in place like a purpose, goals, willingness to struggle and grow, and they don't give up, but they don't have a plan of action because they underestimate the power of writing things down and then following it with discipline. It sounds so simple, right? Just write down some things, some goals, or some to-do's and then having the discipline to get it done consistently. Planning is a skill and should not be taken lightly. Planning and preparation can make an amateur look like a professional. How do you think I got to this point? It's not because of my natural abilities! You may have purpose, passion, preparation, performance, patience, persistence, and perseverance, but if you don't have that other "P" word, Planning, you will probably not succeed. These are what I call the 8 P's of Success.

Again, for most people and in most professions, they already know their job well enough to succeed in it. They don't have to be the best at everything. They just have to make some simple tweaks to their game. They just have to make some minor adjustments to their preparation or their follow-up methods. It could be as simple as waking up 30 minutes earlier to go over their goals, schedules, and plan for the day, then after work, instead of just calling it quits, they take 30 minutes to prep for the next day or make an extra 5 to 10 phone calls a day. Perhaps you could wake up earlier and go workout so that you're always refreshed, full of adrenaline, and become more assertive in closing transactions. Perhaps instead of only making 4 Face to Face calls a day, you make 8 FTF calls a day. Think of some little tweaks you could try out each day, BUT stick to it with conviction until it becomes second nature, and you'll be amazed at the results you will be able to achieve. Believe me, never underestimate the power of small little tweaks to your game. For me, the simple and sustained change that I made to my game that did wonders for me professionally and personally was the laying out of all my clothes for the next day and prepping all my scheduled call items into little manila folders for each call. It saved me so much time having to prep and rush out the door in the morning for my calls. It gave me more clarity and peace of mind than I could imagine a simple little routine like that could ever do. I left earlier for appointments as well, meaning I wasn't stuck in much traffic, didn't have to panic and make apologetic calls, and during my sales calls, I didn't come off hectic and I didn't miss a lot of important details. I was happier, more confident, and as a result, closed more deals. It was simply amazing and eye-opening in hindsight. I went on to further improve little things in my life like keeping my hair short to save time on hair-care and grooming. You thought it was only because I was balding? No! This is by design! It took me years to carefully design this look! And I kept my wardrobe to similar colored polo shirts and simple grayish-black slacks so that I could just grab the top and the bottom quickly and go without ever having to think about it. I would carry an extra packing cube set of clothes in my car as precautions in case I had to go somewhere far for work. I did whatever was required of me to improve myself, my results, and the quality time I have with the people in my life. Otherwise, you're like most average people with average results. You wake up at the last possible time, you hurry up and get dressed and grab a quick bite, you hurry up and get in traffic, then you hurry up and clock in at the last possible minute to be considered on time, then you go to the water cooler or make your rounds to say hi to all your co-workers, then sit down and get ready to work, but by that time, 30 minutes to an hour has passed by. Then you'll hurry up and go straight into the rat race routine of trying to do everything, trying to multi-task, putting out fires, taking care of customers, dealing with complaints and issues, run, run, run, reacting all day, and never getting ahead. You may stay a little later if you have to, but most of the time, well before that, you're already looking at the clock. Then you hurry up and get back into traffic to come home. Then you get home and hurry up and try to catch up to what your wife and kids wanted you to do that you are probably long overdue at. Then you crawl to bed. Not a single brainwave was used to plan, prepare, and focus on what you really need to do to be successful. That's what average people do. If you don't want to be average, don't do what average people do. I repeat, don't do what average reps do.

You don't have to re-invent the whole game to be a good sales rep, you just have to be really good at one or two things. You just have to take one or two things and run with it. I've seen many different types of reps succeed and none of them are really good at all things. That's almost impossible anyway. It's kind of like that Multi-Purpose Primer that I used to sell. We used to call it, The Primer That's Okay For Everything, But Good For Nothin'. You just don't have the time nor the energy to be good at all things. But you can be really good at one thing that is unique to you and is suited to your particular skill-set. I've seen reps succeed by just delivering paint in their cars all day, running around like a glorified, expensive delivery boy, but they are really good at it – they go to lots of job sites, see things other people don't, and are always on top of things. Me, I hate making deliveries, I don't make deliveries, I don't bail out my stores because they will expect it and they will always drop the ball, and I will always have to give up what I'm doing to go deliver paint for them. That's not what I'm good at. I'm not an expensive delivery boy. But I've seen it work. I've seen some reps do nothing but network at events, take all the credit and the splits, and delegate everything else out. They're just really good at schmoozing. I've seen some reps make only 1 or 2 quality calls a day, really well planned and really aggressive on those few calls, but they get results. I've also seen reps who are not really good at anything else, but they like making a lot of face to face calls. They show up a lot and are always top of mind for most customers. If you really think about it, this works the best for most reps. You don't have to be good at prospecting, product knowledge, communication skills, follow-ups, objection handling, or closing, you just have to show up a lot and customers will always think of you and throw you bones and orders when they need stuff because you're always there, while the competitors are not picking up their phones or not showing their faces as often – outta sight, outta mind right? In fact, I know a rep which I will call Kevin Dee, who nobody even likes because he's such an a-hole, but customers still give him business because they know him, they know what he can do, and he's always there. Me, personally, if I had to pick absolutely one thing to choose from, I'm just good at making friends – entertaining. I do most of my business outside of business hours, on the golf course, at the customers' houses or places of entertainment, doing the same hobbies as they do. If I don't know how to do something, I make it a point to go learn it, apply my basic principles of getting good at anything, and become proficient enough to hang with them. How do you think I got good at golf? Because my top customers play golf! When I first became a rep, I didn't know how to golf or bowl. Many of my customers loved these hobbies so I dedicated myself to learning it. I picked it up quickly and got competent enough at it to hang with the pros fairly well. It took a lot of time and money outside my normal working hours, but it was something I believed in. I can shoot the breeze with the best of 'em for as long as it takes. I bombard customers with my presence. Love me or hate me, when they need me, they call me and I answer my phone quickly and deliver on my promises. I was All In. I may not be the number one option yet, but eventually I will be because I'm always there for them. They know all about me and I know all about them. I'm not some unknown, scared young pup or some grumpy old schmuck. I'm damn good at my job. It takes a toll on my family life but I've worked it out with my wife and she understands. Customers know me well and I'm generally a very likeable guy, not to toot my own horn, but I recognize that this is a strength of mine. I've done the math, measured my ROI, and taken the necessary time to study myself truthfully and work on myself on the skills I'm lacking. I'm educated enough and keep up with the times and business news enough to be able to talk to CEO types, and I've been poor enough to hang out with the lowest workers, in fact I've been lower than most people. With the exception of my own family, I don't know too many people who have had to endure such extreme poverty and struggles like me. That one skill of being willing and able to make friends from all walks of life, in combination with my belief in some basic sales principles and a simple solid plan, is why I succeed.

Others may have everything else, but no purpose so they just go round and round, getting nowhere. Others may have everything but perseverance so they quit every time it gets too hard. The point is, most people only need to tweak a couple of things to be successful. There's no secret, luck, or fancy stuff involved. What separates the top five percent from the rest is not some super power that they have and you don't. Just like what separates Lebron James, arguably the best basketball player in the world right now, from the second best player is a small margin – a few rings, something like .5 points in scoring average, 1 rebound average, 1.5 assists average, .25 steals average, and .25 blocks. That's it, very slim margins! And he makes the big bucks, gets all the advertising, the commercials, the deals, the fans, and the haters.

Another example is pro golfers' winnings in tournaments. The winner may have only won by one stroke in a play-off, but he takes home something like $1 million dollars more than second place in a big tournament. From second to third is an equally drastic drop off, and so on and so forth.

The same thing applies to most things in life like sales reps or managers or marriages or anything else. You don't need to make drastic changes. Most people only need some sustained simple tweaks. One thing or change done consistently with purpose and focus will usually yield very powerful results."

I told Gordon, "Dude, from my point of view, you just don't have a purpose to selling paint. You don't know why you're selling paint. You don't know your #truth! So because you don't believe in what you're doing, you don't have the conviction to make the sale, and ultimately you will keep not hitting your budget. How can you? The customer can smell it coming from a mile away and they won't buy what you're selling. You're getting pulled in every direction like most reps – emails, reports, complaints, putting out fires, waiting, issues, problems, life, wife, kids, etc., etc. You don't focus enough in any area to achieve great results in each. Am I right? You're a relatively new rep, relatively new husband, relatively new father, relatively new to the paint game, relatively good, but also relatively bad. I get it, I was there. All you need is to be All In on yourself.

Trust me. All you need is a powerful reason, a why, a purpose…then combine that with a simple plan of action. That's it!

Don't be like all these other chump reps that just take the path of least resistance each day. Whenever they get in front of the prospect, they throw everything but the kitchen sink at the customer, hoping something will stick. Prices, pew! Quality products, pew! Best service in the world, pew! Free demos, pew! Free deliveries, pew! Deals, pew! Cheap, cheap, cheap, pew! Then the customer says no or says they'll think about it, they give the customer their business card and tell the customer, "Call me if you need anything." When the hell has somebody ever called you back when you just give them your business card? It's not even worth the cost of the business card if that's your whole game plan. So then what happens normally? They go to the next customer and do the same thing. The whole time not going after any real prospects, not filling their funnel, not building relationships, just hoping for that customer who is going to land in their lap already walking into the store to buy material – the only thing they could do now is hope to not piss off the customer with their checklist of questions they've been taught to throw at the customer but not believe in it."

At this point, he is amazed and sees his own parallels as I once did. Then I slap him with the #truth. "Bro, let me ask you this, have you ever heard of Brian Tracy, or Zig Ziglar, or Joe Girard, or Stephen Covey, or any of the top sales guys in the world?"

The answer was a blank shaking of the head.

"I didn't think so. You say you really want to be a good sales rep, but you spend most of your time doing the same thing over and over, not doing anything different, hoping by pure chance that you ever have a good year. You say you really want to be a great sales rep but you never spent a single dime or any second researching sales, watching videos about sales, and studying about sales and the top sales people in the world. That's kind of like wanting to play basketball or golf or do anything at a high professional level and then just going out and competing without ever practicing, playing, or knowing anything about your profession or who the best players in the world are. You've got to put in the time and the money. You've got to study the top people in your field. You've got to pay for outside sales seminars and lessons. You've got to get better. You've got to keep learning and growing. You've got to measure yourself. You've got to understand some of the basic principles of your profession – such as dribbling, rebounding, defense, and shooting is to basketball. In sales, it's the 80/20 rule, overcoming fear, preplanned calling, building relationships, and massive follow-up. If you don't know any of what I'm talking about, you need to go straight home and Google these subjects. You've got to be All In to become great at what you do for a living. And you call yourself a professional?

Now, let's get down to the most basic principles of sales for you if truly want to be good at it. Do not underestimate these principles. Let me give you a back drop on these principles. One of my best friends, Lu, and his mom, real estate agents, mediocre, they were down at the bottom of the sales totem pole. Why am I telling you this? Whether you like it or not, sales is important. Everybody in any business is a sales professional. And real estate is one of the toughest sales games in the business. All commission. No salary plus bonus. If you don't sell, you don't pay your mortgage, like most industries. They went to a weeklong real estate training seminar conducted by one of the best real estate training professionals in their industry. $10,000 each. That meant $20,000 for both. They believed in it that much. They spent the money and took the time. It was worth it because otherwise, without anything different, they would be out of business within 2 years of registering as real estate agents. Long story short, I went to knock on his Century 21 office one weekday as I normally do, to pull him out for a round of twilight golf, he lifted the blinds and gave me the five minute hand signal. He came out and said, "I can't go, Dude." I was like, "What? You're gonna miss your weekly ass-kicking? What could be more important?" I will never forget these words, he said, "I gotta stay until I finish making these 100 cold calls." That sentence still comes up every single time I talk about sales. "What gives? Is it that stupid sales training seminar you went to last week?" I asked. He said yes and proceeded to tell me all about it. After about fifteen minutes of description, what I got from it was this: He needs to make 100 cold calls a day to generate about 4 showings a week and massive, massive follow-ups so he can get those 2 closes a month to survive. The best real estate agents in the world make over 200 cold calls a day easy.

That's when I thought about my own business. I came to the conclusion that if I applied the same principles of one of the toughest industries in the business to my own industry, I would be successful as well. At first, it was obviously tough. I hated cold-calling. I dreaded knocking on doors. It was easy when I was a store manager and customers came to me already in the mood to buy. My only job is to not screw it up and just service the hell out of them. It's an entirely different game to go to the customers' environment and sell to them. So I started to apply these sales principles. However, I had to fight through all my fears first. As I told you, it was extremely hard, especially for me, because of my culture and the experiences I had growing up about looking people in the eye. Every time I looked at someone in the eye, especially someone older, I would hear my grandpa and feel him slap me upside the head saying, "It's disrespectful to look at an elder in the eye!" It took me almost a year to overcome that. It was easier once I realized that I was valuable to them and I just had to convince them of it. But that was almost impossible if I didn't get to know them and they knew nothing about me. I had to find creative ways get the customers to notice me. I had to get their attention one way or another. I knew all these things. I read a few sales books regarding learning about a man's motivation before closing them. I knew about the 80/20 Rule already because I applied it to my store manager job and it actually worked. The only problem was I never tried to put these principles into practice so I didn't believe in the principles. There is a difference between knowing and believing. Fear was always looming. Doubt was always in every single one of my conversations. Excuses were just around the corner. Inevitably the objections and rejections would show up. When you don't believe, the prospective customer will be able to sniff it out immediately and you will have very little success. I had to get creative. I hated rejections so that's why I was never good at getting girls' numbers, unlike some of my natural English-speaking tall, blond, and blue-eyed friends. It forced me to take an inventory of what I was good at and started to measure them in a systematic way. I wrote stuff down. I over-prepared and found out that the more prepared I am the more confidence I got, the better I sounded, and the more sales I got. I would always show up at least 15-30 minutes earlier for every meeting, recite what I want, go over some key points, practice my pitch, motivate myself, calm my mind, calm my heart, and calm my fears. Then I would tell myself that even though I wasn't born in this country, even though English was my second language, even though I started so late, I had overcame so much more than most people and I will succeed. Soon I developed a system that was especially suited to my strengths – and to most people for that matter. That year the results spoke for themselves. I got the highest award for sales reps, got my free trip incentive, and got my bonus money. I promised myself I will always keep getting this award because now I believe. I believe in something strongly enough, I owned up to who I really was – good or bad – was All In and did what was required of me to get the job done.

See, most sales reps, like yourself, know what it takes to sell. They just don't believe it because they don't have a purpose, a why, to do what they should be doing. They get pulled in every direction in their job – much like in life. Their results are always mediocre."

A year later, Gordon, finally finding his reason for selling. It was for his kid, he decided. He finally hit budget and is on his way to getting the highest award every year at his company. Another bonus: no more corrective action plans from his boss every other six months. In every walk of life, every industry, every role, and every job, you must believe. There's a difference between knowing and believing.

I've always wanted to own my own business, even when I was in the refugee camps. I would always stare out through the barb-wire fence to see the Thai caravans walking by in the distance, going to the market somewhere to peddle their food, trinkets, and wares. I always wanted to be like them. My dad had the opportunity to guard a Thai shop in the refugee camp on some occasions and I would beg him to take me with him to watch the shop at night. The shop was basically a small convenience store filled with soft-drinks and candy. Of course, I couldn't have any, we couldn't afford any, but I was desperate and content to just be close to them, stare at them and touch them. I'd wish that one day I could get to eat them and drink them every day…one day. And even better, one day I was going to have my own business and have all this Pepsi, Coca-Cola, Sprite, Orange stuff, and candies. I begged my dad so much that he actually took me a couple of times. The best part was when my dad found a plastic bag, filled it up with water, and froze it in the popsicle freezer and give me the frozen ice water bag in the morning. Man, I was the coolest kid in the whole camp the next day. I took them to all my friends and cousins, and we'd make a hole in the plastic bag and take turns licking the ice for what seemed like all freaking day. It was the closest to ice cream I ever had. Those were some of the best days of my 8 years in the refugee camps. So even at an early age, I've always known that I would own my own business. That was my dream coming to America as well as taking showers in Pepsi. I always knew but I never believed. I never took the chance. I was always too scared. Year after year after year, I would always make excuses and say, next year. It was only when I had my first son, wanting to leave a legacy, all my friends had moved up and out or getting forced out, the company was going in a different direction than what I had grown up with, the new bosses – mostly younger than me – were pressuring me to take up more responsibilities, that I started seriously looking for a way out. I was getting miserable. It was building up to a perfect storm. I knew I had what it took to be a good business man, but I didn't believe and I didn't take the chance. Then because of Keng, I finally started to believe in my dreams again and became All In.

Chapter 13 #Truths

- There's a big difference between knowing and believing. Knowing doesn't cause action. Believing causes massive action and results.
- The #truth of your beliefs is where you put your time and money in
- Time and money are two of the most important things to people
- If you believe enough, you will put in whatever time and money to accomplish it
- If you don't believe enough, you will put in only excuses and reasons as to why you can't accomplish it
- Human nature is a good indicator of the future
- Success is not a secret
- You always find time and money for the things you really love
- Success is really simple
- You just have to believe, plan your work, work your plan, show up, focus, focus, focus, and succeed.
- Focus
- Align your thoughts, emotions, words with your actions for success
- You already know mediocrity and suffering, stop holding on to it, go be great
- You don't need to make huge changes. Simple tweaks to your game, done consistently will yield powerful results
- You already have what it takes in you
- Don't underestimate the skill of planning
- Don't do what average reps do.
- Don't try to reinvent the wheel, just do better than other people.
- Don't try to be the best at everything, it's impossible, you'll end up being good for nothin'
- Know your game, know the players, know the basic fundamentals, and don't go home until you're done with work
- Find your reason and be All In on it

Chapter 14: Walkers vs Clappers

When I started in the sales game I noticed one thing above all else. The people who never walked on stage to receive rewards, the people who are perpetually at the bottom of the sales numbers reports, the people who were always clapping for other reps, and the people who move from company to company but never doing anything special are always the ones who made the most excuses about why they can't walk on stage. It's always the economy, or the system is rigged, or their boss is an asshole, or other reps are stealing their accounts, or their products are priced too high, or they don't have certain competitive products to compete, or their services and support teams are always dropping the ball, or their budgets are too high, or their customers have closed shop, or the weather, or any number of things as to why they can't sell. They are so caught up in why they can't sell that they never stop to figure out how they can sell. It was always somebody else's fault or something else was to blame.

On the surface some of these reps seem to have it all going on. They look the part, dress the part, talk the part, and have the experience and industry and product knowledge to have you fooled that they might actually be good reps. I've known some reps that are the best I've ever seen at the things I wish I was that good at, like prospecting, resolving objections, and closing. Sometimes I just stand there with my mouth open in awe at the way they can dance around the customer like they were born to do this. But why is it that year after year after year, they are always flat, always near the bottom or middle of the pack, and always clapping? It could be that they had some early success and that actually boosted their ego to the point that they think they're too good to learn anything new. I think this is one of the worst mistakes that a sales rep could make early on, is to have immediate sales success. Many people might have told them that they were great at the beginning when they first started – too many pats on the back – so they are unknowingly still living in those days while the sales game has long passed them by. I know many a rep who do nothing but talk about the good ol' days 25 years ago when everything was fun, the rules were laxer, and the money was rolling. They love to tell me how great everything was back then when sales reps were real sales reps. They can't learn new things. They fight every change that the company mandates. They complain and spread cancer about every initiative and program. And the ones that piss me off the most, they preach that working hard is beneath them because they've put in the time and are now smarter than everyone else or too good to work hard because they only work smart. Their ego just won't let them do what it takes to sell. It could be that they think they're better than they really are. It could be that they've just never had to overcome much obstacles in their sales career so they never had to struggle and grow. It could be that they're just lazy. Or it could be that they're just shady used-car salesmen types, going around trying to rip people off – I've seen plenty of those too. But mostly, it's because they never took ownership. They never owned the #truth. Owning it means taking responsibility for all your successes and especially your failures. When one takes ownership, no matter where they are at right now, they will develop the mentality, accountability, adaptability, skills, traits, behaviors, habits, and character it takes to succeed. All the denial, excuses, problems, obstacles, resistance, and blame goes out the window. There will only be room for incre-Mental growth and success. It is only through ownership that you will be able to do what it takes to succeed in beating the odds in sales.

Even at the beginning, when I didn't know anything about anything about sales, I was still able to piece out that of all the people who make the most excuses about their jobs or their performances are always the worst reps in the company. Their names are never mentioned in the same breath as the top performers. Don't get me wrong, they may be great guys, fun to hang out with, great to shoot the breeze with over some beers, but they are always the ones clapping year after year for the top performers who are always walking on stage. I remember someone telling me early in my career that there are only two types of people at our company, Walkers and Clappers. Right now, you have to decide, am I a Walker or am I a Clapper?

Managers and reps who seem to constantly walk the stage year after year to receive their top awards are Walkers. They are normally the most positive people with great attitudes. They normally don't complain about things they can't control. They are always sure that they will hit not only hit their budgets but will surpass it, no matter how high the budget has been set or how many years in a row they've hit their ever-escalating budget. However, there is no question about the one thing Walkers do that Clappers don't is that Walkers always have a plan to get on stage again and they do whatever it takes. They are always All In. They expect it and they demand it, because they know their business and they have a solid plan of action of how to get the success they believe they deserve. They believe they are entitled to it, it's their right; thus, they do not take No for an answer. They will not quietly go away from a customer, from their superiors, or even from their peers when a conflict or compensation is in question. They don't make excuses for their performance. They don't focus on what everyone else is doing, they only focus on their plan. Their plan won't allow them to give up so easily and they will do whatever it takes to get the results they are looking for. They may have a big fat ego – don't get me wrong, anyone who is successful usually has a healthy ego – but they use their ego as a motivational, competitive tool that gives them the edge they need to overcome any odds placed in front of them, instead of a crutch that holds them back from learning, growing, and achieving great results. Thus, they always win when going head to head against a competitor or anyone else in their way. That's why they are Walkers, year after year.

Of all the traits that a Clapper has, not having a plan has to be number one on the list. We called it a Sure-plan at The Paint Company, here at Behr, we call it a Territory Growth Plan, some call it a Territory Business Plan. There's a certain test I use to see if store managers are Walkers or Clappers. I just walk into any store and ask where their business plan is. The bad stores and perpetually bad managers will not be able to find it. They will fidget, look around, open random drawers, and say it's somewhere on the computer so they'll have to pull it up. A few may have to think a little bit, pull it out from some dirty drawer somewhere, dust it off, and hand it to me. That's a clear indicator that they haven't looked at it since they presented it to their managers at the beginning of the year and they don't intend to look at it again until they have to make a new business plan to present it to the boss again for the upcoming year.

I equate this to most people and their New Year's resolutions.

The Scene:

December 31st. Again. Everyone is festive, celebratory, and hopeful. Everyone is asking everyone else what their hopes, dreams, and goals are for the coming year. The TV is on showing Ryan Seacrest interviewing celebrities about what they want to do for the upcoming year. Everyone is asking each other what their resolutions are.

"I want to stop smoking cigarettes!"

"I want to quit drugs and alcohol!"

"I want to lose 20 pounds!"

"I want to be toned!"

"I want to finally open up my own business!"

"I want to learn how to dance!"

"I want to learn how to paint!"

"I want to travel more!"

"I want to spend more time with my family!"

"I want to bonus this year!"

"I want to walk the stage next year!"

The list goes on and on and everyone is happy and excited. Then they crawl to bed inebriated. Most will wake up with a hangover and forget about their resolutions and their plans. Some will be motivated enough to start their plans then quit as soon as life hits them again – the wife or husband is mad, the kids got sick, the boss is calling, stress, tired, busy, problems, life – and they quit within days. Some will be motivated enough to keep up their plans for a week, but the effort, discomfort, pain, and soreness is too much and they quit. Some will do it for a month or two at the most, won't see any real results, then quit. The next time they look at their plan again is around New Year and they proceed to make the same resolutions. Year after year, the results are the same.

How can you truly accomplish your plan when you only look at it once or twice a year? That's not a plan, that's just a wish. Not only that, it's not even a very good specific wish. Like my cousin, Mang, told me, his resolution was to be toned. Toned? What does that even mean? You don't even know what that even looks like to yourself. Be Specific. You must be more specific than that if you want something bad enough, otherwise it's just a wish. Wishes and dreams don't work unless you do. There's no genie. The only genie is you. For a plan to work, you must look at it more than twice a year. In fact, what I've seen is that, at a minimum, you must look at it at least once a month to gauge where you are and make the necessary adjustments. The normally successful Walkers look at their plans once a week at least. The real pros look at their plans every single day and tweak it as necessary. Their goals don't change if the results aren't going as planned, they instead adjust their plans accordingly. They believe in what they want and in their plan. They own it. And again, when you own it, you will develop the necessary tools, skills, and habits that it takes to get the results you're looking for. It was already done, now they just have to go do it.

As I got better and went through all my progressions as sales rep and sales manager, I finally understood what it took to be successful. I need to always own where I am at, good or not, no matter where and what stage I am at, and develop the necessary purpose, passion, plan, preparation, performance, perspiration, patience, and persistence that it takes to succeed, and then just don't quit until I achieve it. I've developed a system for success after so many failures. I don't get better by luck or chance. I get better by knowing what I want, making a plan to get it, being All In on it, re-writing my plan over and over every single morning that I wake, going out and working that plan, and then re-checking it every night before I got to sleep. Through this simple method, I have ensured that I am getting better incre-Mentally, one mountain a day.

Without a plan and a system of how to get there, you are relying entirely on chance that you'll be successful. It would just be by pure luck that you hit your goals if there's no plan in place, no preparation, no practice, no measurements, and no purposeful and consistent execution. Just like in golf, you must have a plan of how you're going to navigate the course to accomplish your goal otherwise you'll just be all over the place or as we like to call it, "The Shit." You'll be in the shit all day, every day, for the rest of your life if you don't have a plan. If you somehow do manage to get to the hole, you'll be absolutely exhausted and you won't want to ever experience that again. A plan reduces the amount of swings you take at something and gets you results faster with less effort. This applies to life, business, parenting, marriage, sports, or almost anything else.

Never underestimate the power of a simple, measurable, plan of action. It does not to be precise and rigid, but it needs to be clear and specific. It also helps to be flexible and fun. Amateurs always underestimate planning. It may be the most underestimated skill there is, writing stuff down and planning. The masters don't underestimate it, so why should you? Most amateurs think they can just remember a bunch of stuff in their heads and they think that if they just jot it down on a Post-It note or scrap paper or on their note app in their phone that it'll be sufficient enough. How has that been working out for you? How many times have you forgotten about it, lost it, laundered it because it was in your pant pocket, or never looked at it again? Out of sight, out of mind. When there's too many things to focus on, you end up focusing on nothing. Your mind is jumping all over the place, only stopping to react to what's right in front of you and what's the most urgent at the moment. And their sales or life results are a direct reflection of that too. What you don't focus on won't grow. What you don't focus on you don't care about and you most certainly won't put in the time and money it takes to succeed. Write it down. Get it out of your head. Put pen to paper. Get rid of all the unnecessary shit. Focus.

If you don't have a plan, that's okay, as long you own up to that fact. But believe you me, a plan is crucial. Without a plan, you will wander through life aimlessly. If you achieve success and get to walk the stage at your company sales meeting or the stage of life, it will be by pure dumb luck. Without a plan, you're all over the place and have to deal with too many distractions at your job or in life that it will take you too long, if ever, to get to where you want to go, if you even know where you want to go. The quickest path from point A to point B is usually a straight line. That's what a plan provides for you. Without it, it will be by accident that you ever get what you want…if ever. Own it, be All In, and get a plan and be a walker, or keep blaming and making excuses, and don't make a plan, and be a clapper.

Chapter 14 #Truths

- In sales, there's only two types of people: Walkers and Clappers.
- Walkers find a way
- Clappers find excuses.
- Successful people own it.
- Successful people always have a plan and work their plan religiously
- The quickest path from point A to point B is an All In straight line.

Chapter 15: Stop Listening to the Haters

Who are the haters? Haters are anyone that knowingly or unknowingly discourages you from what truly makes you happy. Haters are not just strangers, critics, or enemies. In fact, they can be your own family, friends, fellow reps, coworkers, anyone, and sometimes haters can be you yourself. The ones closest to you are normally the worst kind of haters because you tend to listen to them more than what's good for you – knowing that they love you and that's why they are doing what they do. They're always in your business or telling you that what you're doing is stupid or crazy. Now, this is where it might get a little tricky if you're new to the sales success game, if you aren't sure what direction you want to go in life yet, if you're still trying to figure out who you are and what you want, or if you're still living at home without a plan. It is crucial that you work on this otherwise the haters will run you around and set you back.

I know they mean well, but even my parents were haters. They and every single one of my uncles and aunts wanted me to be a doctor. Doctors are probably the most prestigious titles in our culture next to government leaders. Doctors represent the most elite class that my people aspire to become. It represented peak education, knowledge, skills, money, influence, and power. I was the valedictorian, one of the oldest first-generation kids in the whole extended family so all the hopes and dreams of the family rested on me. Just because I excelled in school, they all assumed I was going to take on the mantle and study to become a doctor. I had every intention of becoming a doctor – never one to shy away from pressure – but I never really liked school and I quickly found out after taking a bunch of physics, biology, chemistry, and calculus classes that if I had to take 20 more of these types of classes I would have to shoot myself. By the time I decided I hated anything to do with 8 more years of schooling, almost two years had gone by, and my scholarship was going to run out in another two years. That meant I had to fit more than three fully loaded years into two years – summer, fall, winter, spring, summer, fall, winter, spring – just to finish. I'll be damned if my parents had to pay for my college tuition. I'm not blaming anyone but myself for listening to the haters when I knew from the beginning being a doctor wasn't going to make me happy. I just had to own the #truth, be All In, and do whatever it took to graduate.

Even my brother thought that I was crazy. He didn't approve of me using our parents' money as a loan to help fund my partner and me. My brother told me before-hand that I was taking advantage of my parents and trying to manipulate them, and I better know what I was doing. As it turned out, I didn't know what I was doing. Admittedly, I did blame him for a long time because his words seared into my brain and stayed there during my business and for a while after I had failed. Every time I thought about the business and got angry, it would eventually lead to the words he said to me, "I know what you're doing, Bro, and I don't appreciate it. I don't like what you're doing to our parents. They worked so hard for that money. You better know what you're doing. When you fail, I'm not gonna like it."

"When you fail" still burns to this day sometimes when I'm not paying attention and my mind wanders. It hurt. It still hurts sometimes. I know he said those things out of love and concern. I know he loves and respects our parents so much, that's why he said it, but it doesn't the make go away any quicker.

Ultimately, though, I had to take responsibility for everything. I deserved it, good or bad. It was then and only then, that I was able to move on to be All In on my dream. It was an expensive lesson but it catapulted me into the life I now enjoy. It would not have been possible had I listened to him – my very own brother. My little brother who looked up to me and believed I could do anything when we were young, who went on to get his

Ph.D., who saw me lose my way, give up on my dreams, struggle, suffer, defer to my wife for all decisions, and saw clearly that I wasn't going to succeed in anything because I didn't have what he saw when we were young anymore. He saw I wasn't All In. Perhaps one day he'll look up to me as he once did. Things change and things will always change. For now, I can only afford to focus on being All In on my dreams.

I blamed him because I couldn't handle and own the #truth. I couldn't even look at myself in the mirror most of the time. It was much easier to blame and hate. Who does he think he is? I protected him all those years when he was a skinny little sickly boy. I would never question anything he does. He must have forgotten all the things I had to overcome growing up with him, being the older brother and the guinea pig for all the experiments in America by my parents. I gave him up for good for a little while. I expressed to my mom that I was done with him. So be it. I'll show him that I'm not done yet and when I do, he will be the first one I call out. My mom cried and pleaded. I decided I didn't need anyone as long as I got my two boys. Inevitably though, when I started thinking about my boys and how great they are together, it would always lead back to how great my brother and I were when we were young. Five and three, exactly two years apart like my brother and me. The big one was always showing the little one everything, what to do and what not to do, always looking out for each other. Nothing in this world would ever compare to that. It would kill me to see them break up over some stupid, meaningless words in the past. Thanks to my Dad, I got my senses back.

All my friends, my family, my wife, everyone, thought I was crazy. They were right. I had to be crazy because normal wasn't getting it done. Once you've tried all other avenues of normal and nothing worked, sometimes you just have to be crazy to get the results you want. The point is nobody knows you better than you do. Your loved ones may want what's best for you, but they don't know your deepest darkest fears, truest desires, and what you believe in. Sometimes you don't even know yourself. They just don't want you to get hurt and suffer. But you are the only one who knows what you truly want, what you have to do, and what it's going to take to get there. Nobody will do your push-ups for you so stop asking for permission.

Easier said than done, I know. These days pretty much everyone will agree that with social media, the haters are everywhere. If you've got a big enough account, you will not be able to post anything without the haters and trollers having something negative to say about it. Most try to create a persona for others to see and admire. They put on their best pictures, usually with tons of make-up, filters, or touched up by Photoshop. They are always going out, traveling, having fun, eating foods, hanging out, and looking pretty and happy all the time. Nobody really posts the bad stuff unless it's bad, and even then, most people will question the motive because so many just do it for sympathy and attention. Just look at any picture from a popular person and there will be thousands upon thousands of bickering back and forth and just outright hate. The Haterade is strong on Social Media because people can say what they want while remaining relatively anonymous or unhinged. In society, though, it's just not that cool to say it, especially regarding politics. Nobody wants to hear anything about what the other side is saying, whether it makes sense or not, just because of the messenger. If you are one or all of these, you may be a hater.

The purest and most noble deeds in the world are not immune to the hate and criticism. Martin Luther King, Jr. had his haters. Here was the face of the Civil Rights Movement, incredibly prolific, believed in his cause enough to die for it, and his haters were saying he should be more like Malcolm X, be less passive, and be more violent. The reverse goes for Malcolm X as he was apparently too violent and dangerous for many people's tastes. Gandhi had his haters, a man that changed the lives of millions of Indians and influenced so many others around the world. Even

Mother Teresa had her haters. Here was a woman who devoted her entire life to helping the poor. She was in the gutters, the ditches, and the trenches of poverty and leprosy while her haters sat on their couches, in their comfortable homes, watching TV, reading about her, and throwing darts at her. When it comes down to it, all they could do was hate and say she should have done it this way or that way. Here's the kicker, if you were to ask every single one of those haters to go out into the gutters, get dirty, and help the poor and do as they preach – the answer will always be, "No thanks." That's where the #truth lies, everything else is just hate. You may be a hater.

When I was a teenager, I never understood why my dad never said anything to my grandpa about his temper tantrums. He was always miserable, always smoking cigarettes and spitting luggies into the kitchen sink and not rinsing it off, and always breaking things. He even broke our poor family TV once after an argument with my grandma. My mom would just shake her head in disgust but she never dared utter a single word out of tradition and out of respect for my dad. My dad wouldn't even dare shake his head. He was always dead silent, almost like he never even saw it. After most fights with my grandma, Grandpa would scream out at her, "I buried two wives already, I'm not afraid to bury another one!" My grandma would shut up after that pretty quickly. I always thought it was funny. Years later, after a fight with my own wife, I tried to channel my inner Grandpa and yelled, "I haven't buried any wives before, but I'm not afraid to bury one!" Obviously, the results weren't the same as that of my grandpa; In fact, it had the opposite result I was looking for – an emboldened wife and many a nights on the couch. I never understood why my dad would never say anything to Grandpa. I understood the whole concept of the youngest boy having to shoulder the responsibility of taking care of the parents in our culture, but come on, something had to be said. My dad was always a good kid, never caused any trouble, got picked on by his older half-brothers a lot when they were young, always trying to prove himself to his brothers and his own father, but I never understood why he never had the balls to tell my grandpa to relax in America. I mean, here my grandpa was in America, the Land of the Free, Home of the Brave, The Land of Opportunity, The Land of Giants, and he was miserable. Back in the old country, he was piss poor and experienced nothing but death and tragedy. Here, he should've had no worries and no problems except for his own stubborn unwillingness to want to learn how to drive a car and making my brother walk with him to the convenience store to buy liquor and cigarettes so my brother can make sure the change was correct. He got ripped off one time and vowed never to let that happen again by asking my brother and I to go with him every time. I was never willing to go with him and he absolutely resented me for that. He was a very proud person. He'll never ask you again if you say no. I never cared; in fact, I resented him for being angry and bitter all the time, always reminiscing about the good ole times, and never enjoying his time here in America.

I always hung my hat on the fact that I was very astute at understanding human behavior because I had seen so much growing up. I knew that fear ran my grandpa's life just like most of the elders. My grandpa was my best study in fear. The old country was nothing but death, loss, tragedy, poverty, famine, disease, war, suffering, destruction, running, escaping, hiding dying, and freaking fish bone soup. However, over there, my grandpa was the clan elder. He was looked on with complete obedience and respect for all the things he's seen and all the things he knows. In the old country, he being the oldest, the one with all the knowledge and wisdom, the village leader, the shaman, the keeper of traditions and ceremonies, his words were law, literally in some cases. Everyone had to defer to his knowledge of the culture and customs – nothing gets done without him. Rituals, cultures, customs, knowledge was passed onto the oldest sons and everyone else lived close to them because they were the only ones capable of performing all the rites. I guess that's one way of forcing your legacy to stay close to one another. You can't even look at the elders in the eye because you weren't good enough yet, you don't know anything. Complete and utter respect and obedience was your only duty.

However, in this country, there was an opportunity to be happy. There were no more deaths, wars, poverty, tragedy, and all that other mess. My grandparents, like most elders, never wanted to come to America in the first place. They were forced to obey their kids who wanted to live a better life here. My grandparents used to tell me lies back in the refugee camps. That's why they told me so many lies when I was a six or seven years old so I could tell my parents not to come to America. Who would do such a thing to a kid? Because they didn't want to come to America, even though death, tragedy, and poverty was all they knew. Because that was all they knew and they would rather stick with what they know then something...new. New is unknown. New is uncertain. New is uncomfortable. Even if new is good for you. Even if new is the Land of Opportunity where you can finally be happy for once in your life. Fear is a bitch. I saw it and experienced it first hand to the Nth degree. I thought I was a master of understanding fear.

My grandpa and I never got along and had some bad fights. He once held a knife to my face telling me he created me and isn't afraid to destroy me. I remember it well because it was the closest to death I've ever been. My girlfriend, my first and only, who would later be my wife, was visiting me from Canada and I just didn't bother coming home to help my parents at the farm that week. We stayed at my cousin's apartment in the nearby town. When I finally came home to introduce my girlfriend to the family, my grandpa was angry and told me I was a lazy punk who didn't want to help his parents at the farm. I shot back that he was an angry, bitter, old fart who never cared about our family or my parents. I also reminded him of the fact that he didn't even approve of my parents buying the farm in the first place, and now he's all about helping them which was BS. He ran to the kitchen, grabbed a knife, screamed all the slurs known to my language such as "Tiger Bite!", waved the knife in front of my face, and raising it several times to threaten to chop my head off like a pig as he put it. I dared him like the fool I was and got away with it, with the help of my mom begging for my life. My dad, upon finding out later, would not talk to me for weeks. I don't think I've ever made him that disappointed.

That was the way our relationship was until my grandpa's death in April of 2004 from lung cancer from decades of smoking cigarettes. I'm glad he was able to see me get married before he died. He even performed the Hmong wedding ceremony. My wife and I got married both traditionally at my parents' house and Americanized in Las Vegas – why not - in March of 2004. A month after that he passed away. Before he passed, I was able to come up to see him, cried, told him I loved him, and that I was so sorry for being such a punk. This was the first and only time he ever said he loved me and that I wasn't a punk. He told me not to feel sad for him because he wanted this. He told me to not cry for him and just go on living my life here in America and to take care of my wife and family. I apologized profusely for him to forgive me. He told me that he had already forgiven me a long time ago, that he would look down upon my family and I, and bless us, and that we should not worry about him, because he had lived a full life already and now it was time for me to live mine. The last thing he said to me was that he had buried two wives, nine sons and daughters, all his parents and elders, most of his brothers and sisters, and most of his friends and family, but he knows my life will be different and that makes him happy.

I would think about this moment for over eleven years until recently when my dad slapped me with the #truth about me being an ingrate and pulled me from the pits of my despair back into the light by telling me I didn't know anything about zero.

My dad asked me, "Do you know why I never said anything to your grandpa all those years ago?"

I shook my head like a sad imbecile, then he said, "Because I would never want to even dare to step into your grandfather's shoes for one second, much less a day or his entire life! I love you and your brother more than life itself. I would gladly lay down my life for either one of yours. Think about it, Son. Your grandpa had buried so many sons and daughters! A parent should never have to do that! I can't even begin to imagine what that must be like! That's not including all the other things he had to suffer through! That's why I never said anything to your grandpa all those years ago! Until you are ready to step into another person's shoes, you have no right to say anything to them!"

I finally understood, after all these years, who my grandpa really was at that moment. It only took me 35 years. I also learned another very important thing: World peace would be possible already if human beings would only learn to step into each other's shoes for just one minute. Wars would be averted, suffering would be ended, world hunger would not exist anymore, and world peace would be achieved. If haters would stop hating. Now that I'm a proud parent of two of the most beautiful boys in the world, I realized that I really wasn't astute or had much understanding of fear, human behavior, or my grandpa at all. I was just scared and confused...and I was the worst hater there ever was.

So, if you ever want to do anything worthwhile in life, you must stop listening to the haters and you must stop being a hater. All my years of personal experience of being a hater, I can tell you something about haters. If you don't want any haters, if you just want to be liked by everyone, then you need to live in your parent's basement and never come out, because you're going get your ass kicked out there. The moment you do something right, that's when the haters start coming out of the woodwork. In fact, these days, that's my cue on whether I'm doing something right or not. If there's only love and praise, I know I need to do something else. If there's ever any question, I start asking around or just start listening to the hate, and wherever the hate is the strongest, that's what I know I must do. Criticism is unavoidable. The most successful people in the world have the most hate and criticism. That's a fact. If nobody gives a rat's ass about you then it means you're not up to much of anything. There is nothing you can do that will yield a perfect lovable following of fans. You must make a choice to be something or nothing. If you want to be nothing, listen to the haters and do nothing. If you want to follow your dreams, do what you love, live the life that you are destined to live, be all in, then get ready to face the haters.

Chapter 15 #Truths

- Know your haters, you may be a hater
- Don't listen to the haters, listen to your heart
- Stop asking for permission from others and yourself to do what you want in life
- Be authentic, stop focusing on others
- There is no way to avoid the haters in life
- Until you've walked in another person's shoes, you have no right to tell them what to do

Chapter 16: Actualize Yourself

"Actualize yourself!" – Bruce Lee

Abraham Maslow's theory of the hierarchy of needs illustrates that self-actualization is the highest form of need once all your other needs such as esteem, belonging and love, safety, and physiological are fulfilled. In other parts of the world, the third world where I was from, you probably won't have the opportunity to actualize yourself. Here, you do. As I see war, hunger, suffering, disease, and refugees, I see my people and my struggles, so I see the struggles of the human condition. We are all the same. We all have hopes and dreams. We all suffer. We all just want a better life. That means you should be grateful that you have the opportunity to make the best of yourself. Your only duty in life is to be the best you that you can be, whether that is being the best sales rep you can be, the best parent you can be, the best man or woman you can be, best son or daughter you can be, or any other part of your life. Take time to invest in you. Find out who you really are and what's really important to you. If you don't know yet, you need to spend the rest of your life finding the answer to that question.

The number one problem that holds people back from making the necessary time it takes to actualize themselves is what my father calls Living in LaLa Land. It's all the lies they tell themselves. It's all the time they spend creating their false identity, pretending to be somebody else, and creating a wonderful Facebook or Instagram page for people to see. Most people these days live in Lala Land – the land of make-belief, fairy tales, TV, Social Media, marketing, and propaganda. They have never had an original thought, or if they did, it had long since been smashed to pieces and replaced with what the media and corporations want them to think. They blindly follow and shun what their affiliations tell them even if it's not beneficial to their own personal self-interest. This is especially true when it comes to politics or religion. They've been taught that everything ends like the movies, fairy tales, and TV shows. They've been forced the concept of being romantic all the time. Girls want guys to wine and dine them every single day, be romantic every single day, make them fall in love every single day, and live this rom-com, fairy-tale life. Guys want girls to stay the same as the day they first met them – skinny, wild and crazy, and horny. What have you done for me lately? It's just Lala Land. Welcome to reality. Until you do the necessary things and make the necessary time to work on yourself, and find out what you want in life, you will be stuck in this cultural, societal, media and corporate sponsored Lala Land. It will hold you back more than anything else in life. You will refuse to accept what your true strengths and weaknesses are.

I always believed that my greatest strength was always my greatest weakness.

I was never satisfied with what I had, always reaching for more because I believed I deserved more. That was the seed of all my successes against all odds and the source of all my discontent, suffering, and failures.

In life, you must own the #truth about what your greatest strength is and use it as a tool reach your highest potential. Do not be oblivious to this and go through life haphazardly using this strength as a weapon which could hurt you and others around you.

I knew this one rep, we shall call her, Steel. Naturally gorgeous inside and out, that's without make up on. If she did make herself up...damn. Intelligent. Witty. Great sense of humor. Great at building relationships. And is one of the hardest working people you will ever meet. Her parents were well off so she didn't even need to work if she didn't have to. She'd work so hard and get so dirty that I'd have to tell her to clean her ass up. She was always a top performer at any job she ever worked at. She was a top manager at her former company, my old company. When she came here she immediately became the top store rep at the largest volume and busiest store in the nation and stayed there at the top spot. This girl had so much latent power that everyone she encountered instantly wanted to be near her. Everyone was drawn to that power – her co-workers, friends, bosses…everyone. Every guy around her wanted to be with her. Every time she gets dumped by a dude, we'd all say, that guy is really, really stupid. Her closest co-workers would always say, If Steel ever figures it out, the CEO of this company is in trouble of losing his job. Everyone knew that. Except for her.

See, Steel's number one strength is her undying humbleness. Her number one weakness is also her humbleness. During one conversation when I had an opening for her to be one of my outside sales reps, she asked me, "BOLO, what do I need to do to be a sales rep under you?"

I told her, You just need to tell me that you want the job.

"You don't need to interview me?" she asked in surprise.

"No, I've been interviewing you ever since you came on board," I stated. "I already have all the answers I will ever want from you. The ridiculous results you've been putting up speak for themselves."

I continued, "But you gotta tell me you want it. I only offer this position to people who deserve it, and most of that is wanting it bad enough. That's the only reason you may not get this position. It's because you haven't demonstrated to me that you want this job even though you are the most qualified person for the job. It was always your job to lose. Everyone else is a distant second. You don't know what you want. You don't know who you are. You don't believe in yourself. And you are too afraid to take any risks. You would much rather stay at this position that you've already outgrown because it's comfortable. This was the first time you've ever had a conversation with me about being a sales rep. I've got other people almost calling me every day to be one of my reps. They deserve it more than you because they want it more than you. If you tell me you want it right now, I'd give you the job right now. So how about it? DO YOU WANT THIS JOB more than anything else right now?"

I don't know, was her answer.

"You see, Steel? Your greatest strength is your humbleness. And your greatest weakness is your humbleness."

"You don't even have a clue about what everyone else sees. You are unstoppable and you don't even know it. You would already be way higher than me on the corporate ladder if you'd only recognize the power you have within yourself."

"What do I always ask you, Steel?" I asked.

She replied, "You never ask me any other questions except, What does Steel want?"

Exactly. You can't be All In if you don't know what you want. And you can't actualize yourself if you're not All In. As in Steel and all my reps, it becomes evidently clear that their greatest strengths are always their greatest weaknesses.

There's another rep, we shall call him, Slick, who always preaches, I work smart, not hard. His greatest strength is that he works smart and can get any account to purchase because he thrives on converting tough accounts with his intellect and creativity. However, this is also his greatest weakness. This is why he almost always never makes budget year after year. He just doesn't work hard at all. The accounts realize that shortly after, and eventually the accounts stop buying from him altogether. If he would only own the #truth about himself and work just a little bit harder, he'd be the best rep in our industry.

Another rep, Steve, preaches that he will outwork anyone. He's the best sales rep I had, perpetually number one in the nation. Nobody outworks him. He had no life other than this job, no family, no friends. He doesn't even have an office job and sometimes people would find him at the corporate office hunched over his desk passed out asleep. I got a call one day from my sales admin that I need to tell Steve to give up his desk and clear everything because we were growing and we just hired a couple of new marketing gals so we needed his desk. The whole time I thought it was just a running joke that Steve had a desk at the corporate office! I mean, why would you want to be at the damn corporate office if you could work from home like all of us reps and managers? He was All In on his job, that's why he was the best. Shoot, I'd get emails at midnight and 5 in the morning all the time from him. It's a good thing for him I go to sleep at 12 A.M. and wake up at 4 A.M. to work out every day. But because his greatest strength is hard work, his greatest weakness is that he doesn't work smart. He still hasn't learned to use our CRM system to this day. Everything he does is excruciatingly slow and tedious. A sales call that should take 10 minutes, he overthinks everything and drags everything out. He delivers most of his orders instead of using our company fulfillment resources.

Another rep, Dee, always says, "I will be successful, Bolo, because I don't let people down!"

I told him, "Dee, that's why you'll never be the best, because your greatest weakness is that you never let people down. You give too much crap about what every customer, co-worker, bosses, family, and friends think about you. In order to be the best, you're going to have to stop giving a crap about what people think. You're gonna have to disappoint some people and be perfectly fine with it so that you can focus on what is required of you to be successful."

Another rep, Dan, has the biggest ego of any rep I've ever met. Many of the reps turned down the really big fish accounts in the region because they feared all the hard work it takes to land and service just one of those accounts. To land one of these big fishes, it would take a tremendous amount of time and expense to entertain the owners, estimators, office personnel, foremen, crews, their GC's, and the owners they work for. If you actually manage to land one of these big fishes, then imagine 20 foremen from one company calling you every day with complaints, orders, deliveries, meetings, job walks, issues, and of course, emergencies – at all hours of the day and night. And this guy took over 10 of the biggest fishes in my region because nobody else wanted it. Ten! To date, he actually managed to land 3 of the 10. Not bad at all, but I had to start distributing the rest to other reps because he could not realistically handle all 10 anyway as shown by the results. In fact, those 7 companies didn't want anything to do with him or our company because he just kept dropping the ball. The worst is that he just could not accept that fact. When I finally made a business decision to start taking them away from him, it was the biggest unnecessary clash I'd ever been in. VP's and HR had to get involved because it was ugly. All because of his ego, his greatest weakness. To be clear though, I have a big ego as well. Having an ego is not a bad thing. Your commitment to results and excellence just has to be bigger than your ego. Most people have it the other way around. That's the problem.

So, until you own the #truth, stop listening to the haters, stop living in LaLa Land, accept your greatest strengths and weaknesses, you will never actualize yourself.

It will keep you from truly being able to focus on your true work and to live your most fulfilling life.

I'm not trying to preach to you as if I'm better than you. I've just been there and suffered unnecessarily for a long time. I'm here to tell you to snap out of it. Stop living in LaLa Land. Own your greatest strengths and weaknesses. Own the #truth. Stop blaming circumstances. Stop blaming other people. Stop letting other people and stop letting yourself tell you that you can't do this or you can't do that. Stop lying to yourself. Stop being your own worst enemy. Get out of your own way. Take 200% responsibility and start living the happy, fulfilling, successful life that you deserve. Work on yourself. Do whatever it takes to find out who you are, what's important to you, and what you want to do with the rest of your life. Be All In and actualize yourself.

Chapter 16 #Truths

- Your only duty in life is to be the best you that you can be
- Invest in yourself
- The only question that's important is: What do I want?
- Stop living in LaLa Land, stop lying to yourself, focus on the real you, it's not all romantic all the time like in the movies
- Actualize yourself

STEP 3: Do What's Required

"It is not enough we do our best; sometimes we must do what is required."

-Winston Churchill

Chapter 17: Your Best is Not Enough

Your best has only gotten you to where you are right now. From now on you must do what is required of you to get whatever the hell it is you want and achieve your success that you have within you. What does it mean by doing what is required? Most of the time, doing what's required of you, simply means you just need to keep your word. Like Tony Montana said in the movie, <u>Scarface</u>, "All I have in this world is my balls and my word, and I don't break them for no one!" If you simply stop breaking your own balls about the past and simply do what you say you're going to do, this will create powerful results.

Never underestimate real integrity. Never underestimate the power of keeping your promise. It is perhaps the strongest thing any person can do, especially if they have every reason to not do it…i.e. staying with a wife or husband who has cheated on you because you promised for better or for worse. Many people would see it as weakness, I see it as true strength, the strength it takes to succeed in anything in life. Another less drastic example is promising your wife you're going to do some chores after you get back from work, but you had a long crazy hard day and upon returning home, you're just tired as all hell. I used to just say I'm tired and say I'll do it tomorrow, and end up not doing it most of the time. Without a doubt, the one singular difference I made these last two years that produced the most results in my life besides believing in myself is simply keeping my word, especially to myself, even when I don't feel like doing it. Keeping your word is not for others, it's for you. Normal people do the opposite. They hold others accountable for promises made, but never themselves. That's why nobody believes in people anymore when those people say, I give you my word. I don't want to be normal anymore so I simply do the opposite of what normal people do.

Case in point:

I started writing this book in May of 2015 and promised myself I was going to be done by the end of May 2016. I gave myself a year to do it. I knew it was enough time if I keep my word to myself. Then I got to about 25 pages and moved on to other books, ideas, business, work, wife, kids, and life, and forgot all about it. Thankfully I set a reminder for myself because when my phone dinged at noon on May 8th, 2016, I was immediately re-introduced again, in a state of panic, to my promise. On May 31st, 2016, less than a month, this book was completed. This book, through a tedious revision process when I wanted to impact my Behr Paint Company, went from being about how to achieve the American Dream to this sales book you're reading right now. But how did I do it? Simple. I just kept my word. I didn't break my own balls. I owned up to the fact that I have been slacking off all year but I still had a little time. I went to my wife and had a serious conversation and bargaining session with her to allow me all of May off. She had to bathe, clean, take care of the kids entirely and keep them off me, while doing all the chores and not plan anything that would include me, and just let me do what I need to do. I wrote, day and night, getting only 3 or 4 hours of sleep each night until the book was completed on the last night of the month. Keep your word, it's damn powerful. It is the singular most powerful distinction I ever learned.

Another case in point:

One of my cousins, May, called me up one day after seeing some of my motivational video posts online and asked me how to solve her situation. She explained that she's been trying so hard, but she's just so frustrated and about to give up on her husband. She just doesn't know what to do anymore. Her husband doesn't have a job and just sits at home all day not taking care of the kids while she goes out to work. When she gets home she still has to do all the cooking, cleaning, and all the other chores. She said she regretted marrying a typical Hmong dude who has no job and all he wants to do is fish, hunt, drink, smoke, play poker, and hang out with his friends while neglecting the kids all day. She said her kids are so behind in school that she feels like a horrible mother and now she has developed hatred for her husband as well. May was crying and begging for help. I really didn't know what to do, I've never been in a situation like that before, but I do know about the #truth.

I told her, "May, I don't know the exact situation you're in, I haven't heard his side of the story, and even then, I'll never fully know what is going on, but I know this: I know that YOU KNOW exactly what you need to do, you're just scared, it's really hard, and you just don't want to do it. Most people on this planet know what they need to do, but they don't. See, it's much easier to blame others and your situations in life. I also know if you keep doing the same thing over and over, all you'll get is the same miserable results you've been getting. Is this what you want? What do you want exactly? She hesitated, she couldn't answer. See, you don't even know what you want! First of all, you need to know what you want. What you REALLY want. Then you make it a priority, block out all the noise, and do what is required of you, whatever that is for you.

Most of the time you only have to do two things to get anything that you want in life:

#1) Do what you say you're going to do.

#2) Do what you don't want to do or what others won't.

See, number one means basically keeping your word to yourself and others, keeping your promises to yourself and others, not giving up on what's important to you just because it's hard, and just having real integrity. Again, having real integrity is the most important. To me, having real integrity means keeping your promise at all costs, especially to yourself. When you make a promise to others, it's not really for them, it's for you. Yes, they are the ones benefitting as well, but if you keep the promise, the benefits for yourself are so much more than to others.

And number two means to just do the things you don't want to do even though it's what's required of you just because you're scared, doubtful, hurt, frustrated, angry, mad, sad, sore, don't feel like it, weak in that particular field or area, don't want to deal with it, hard, expensive, and time intensive, or you'd much rather just slack off, procrastinate, be lazy, watch TV all damn day, and any number of things you'd rather do to avoid the things you need to do. Everybody can do anything when it's easy and when they feel like it, but nobody really wants to put in the work to get the results they really want. It's really freakin' hard! Like my mom always said, "If it was easy, everyone would do it." You don't want to be poor? Just do what poor people don't want to do, which is wake up really early, work their ass off, plan, network, save, learn, grow, risk, build, and never give up. Just do the opposite of what poor people do. You want to be fit, same thing, do the opposite of what fat people do which is eat clean, weigh yourself constantly, measure your calories, wake up early, work out consistently and hard even when you're sore, educate yourself, learn about your body, put in a lot of sweat equity, and never give up. I could go on and on about any other thing you want to accomplish in life. If you want to be the best at your work place, just be good at doing all the things that others don't want to do or refuse to do. Come early, handle objections, solve the pesky problems, take responsibility, work with people you don't like, help others succeed, stay longer, do more than what you're paid, and any other number of things. If it was easy, everyone would be fit. If it was easy, everyone would be successful. If it was easy, everyone would be a millionaire. You, specifically, you say your kids are the most important thing? Then do that thing and cut out all the BS! Do what you haven't wanted to do and have been avoiding all this time because it's hard. Of course, it's hard, if it was easy, everyone would still be married, divorces would be non-existent, and there would be only exceptional kids growing up to exceptional adults! So, take some time, May, do what is required of you, be All In."

Four months later, May called me up and said, Thank you. She told me she went All In and quit her job for 4 months to be with her kids and to work on her marriage. I said, so that's why you were posting all those happy pictures of the fam on Facebook, huh? That was exactly right. She said she spent time with the family, made them realize they are the real priority in her life. She taught the kids how to read better, made up with her husband, and her life is better than it's ever been. I didn't need to go into details on exactly what she did step by step or what she plans to do in the future since she may not have a job anymore, because it wasn't important. I knew and she knew that she would always be okay. Don't go play golf, get your nails did, watch movies, play sports, hang out with your friends, drink, fish, hunt, party, club, social media, or anything else when you've got issues at home or with yourself that you haven't owned up to and haven't done what's required to get real results in. Speaking from personal experience, that's just cheating, escapism, or avoidance. Sometimes resolving yourself and your issues is what's required of you to get all the things you want in life.

Sometimes, doing what's required is just sacrificing a little stuff. For most of you, you just need to give up some stuff like your cell phones, video games, TV, social media, and whatever distractions you're into. Some of you need to stop posting "bored" status on Facebook. If you have time to be bored on Facebook, you have time to be successful. Some of you need to give up fishing, gambling, drinking, hobbying, partying, hanging out with your friends, smoking, drugs, alcohol, eating junk food, procrastinating, sleeping so much, or whatever you make time for instead of being successful. Some of you don't just have one or two of these activities, you may have them all. I know I was guilty of most at one point in my life. Have you ever made the time to measure and calculate how many hours you spend doing these activities? You normally don't because you enjoy them and time flies when you're doing these activities and you can't ever get enough. But you just have to start giving it up, because the cost is time and money. You may not need to even give it up entirely, you don't need to become a monk, but you have to know what you want, have your priorities straight, make certain active choices, and do less of these activities until you are successful. If you're not successful yet, you need to focus more on that which you said you will do as opposed to wasting most of your time. For example, you don't need your minimum eight hours of sleep, otherwise you would be successful already just by sleeping. I know, I was one of those who could never sleep enough. If no one woke me up, I'd be able to sleep peacefully until one or two in the afternoon, always needing my sleep, telling myself I need my sleep. When I was all in, I had no choice but to sleep only 4 to 5 hours a night and was able to get more done and get closer to my dreams. I finally understood how my beautiful wife was able to only get a few hours of sleep a night after such a difficult labor and still get up to breast feed my first newborn son and change his diapers in the middle of the night numerous times. The unconditional love of a mother will never cease to amaze me. If you are passionate about something, if you have something great you have to do, sleep wouldn't be an issue anymore. Recent studies on sleep conducted with traditional hunter/gatherer societies have proven that you don't need the 8 to 9 hours of straight sleep a night that everyone says you do to be able to function. Google it yourself for the details. All you need to do is what is required of you to be successful instead of wasting so much time on stuff that doesn't bring you one step closer to success. It's that simple, you have to stop doing your best, do what's required, and start allocating time and money from all your hobbies and your stuff, and funnel that into being All In.

Sometimes, like my parents had to do, it's picking your entire family up and immigrating to a whole new country with nothing but the clothes on your back and not a single red cent to your name, not knowing any of the language, customs, culture, not knowing how to drive, or anything else. The only thing they had was hope.

For some, doing what is required means you might have to ask some really tough questions.

You might want to ask yourself, "Am I really gaining anything where I am right now?" You might want to pick up and go somewhere to get away, get a new perspective, and work on yourself. A change of scenery works wonders sometimes. If nothing else, it will just open your eyes up to all the possibilities out there that you would otherwise not be exposed to. When I was in the refugee camps, I thought the world was flat and there's only one type of white people – tall, blue eyed demons who were waiting to pick me up with chopsticks and stir-fry me. When I was growing up in Northern California, my only options seemed to be to go to Chico State, smoke, drink, party, get someone pregnant, then get a job at the local Wal-Mart. When I came down to Southern California, my mind was blown. Then when I started traveling the world, my mind was blown even more. All because of changes of scenery.

You might want to ask yourself, "Do my parents really know what's good for me?" Your parent's just want what's best for you and they want to protect you, but they don't know what you really want. My wife would still be in Canada not being my wife if she listened to her parents when she told them she wanted to come to the States, live with this guy they don't even know, and pursue her dreams of becoming a fashion designer and of course, marrying me. I've got cousins who still live at home well into their thirties because they keep listening to their parents – always asking for permission to do anything, that's why they still also ask for an allowance. You might want to stop listening to them and do what is good for you. Alternatively, though, some of you might need to start listening to your parents, depending on your situation right now, doing what is required of you.

You might want to ask yourself, "Do I really need all my friends?" Jim Rohn said, "You are the average of the five people you spend the most time with." If five of your friends don't have a job, guess what, you probably don't have a job either. If five of your friends are successful, I'm willing to bet you are successful. So, if you want to be successful and you are not, you might want to consider making new friends. Sometimes through osmosis, you'll just seemingly start thinking differently and doing things differently if all your new friends think differently. If all you and your friends do is hang out every weekend at the clubs, at the bars, playing video games, or just general goofing around, I'm willing to bet that this is who you really are, despite what you profess to yourself and everyone who would listen.

You say you want to be successful? Do what's required of you instead of just dreaming, wishing, and scheming about it. More action, less talk. Speak with your habits, victories, and successes instead of your mouth. Like Nike says, Just do it.

Stop cheating too. Just like in fitness, you want to make it to the professional leagues in fitness and bodybuilding but all you do is cheat. You have cheat meals, cheat days, cheat weeks, cheat months, cheat years – hell, some of you have been cheating all your lives.

When I first started working out and trying to be fit, I was such a cheater. I couldn't afford to cheat because I was overweight but I cheated like I was the fittest person in the world which was ultimately why I failed. What's one donut or cookie, right? What's one Coke? What's one beer? What's the big deal if I skip a couple of days or a week? That's true if you're already fit and have had the discipline and consistency to be fit, but I wasn't. It never stops at one cookie, you know that. I didn't have the right habits yet. I was still fat, and the more I worked out, it seemed to me I deserved to cheat more. In addition, as my metabolism increased a bit, so did my appetite and I over-ate and cheated even more. After two months of being sore and always hungry for no reason, I quit. It's because I was cheating and celebrating before I even made it. I wasn't that good yet.

You are cheating if waking up late and coming home early from your day. You're also cheating if you're celebrating every Thursday, Friday, Saturday, and Sunday or even everyday like you made it already, like I was a long time ago. You just can't afford to. Some of you barely have a car, can barely keep a job, can barely sell a bucket of paint, have no clue what you want, and no plan, yet you celebrate and hang out with your friends all the time, living the life, spending all your time and money chasing the opposite sex, not making time for yourself, not working on yourself or your dreams, just having fun drinking, smoking, partying, fishing, hunting, doing all your hobbies like you have no care in the world. What are you celebrating? You're an amateur, beginner, novice, poor, average, maybe even middle class, or you're not anywhere near where you want to be so you have nothing to celebrate and cheat. You haven't made it yet. You're still living paycheck to paycheck, you're still struggling, suffering, and/or you're still not fulfilled yet so you why are you cheating? Why are you not objectively accepting the #truth, not measuring yourself and your real performance, not meticulously preparing and practicing, not doing what is required of you, and not being All In?

The pros, the seasoned, the masters, and the experts don't cheat and don't take a lot of time off because they know what it takes. They don't underestimate their opponents, their situations, and themselves. They are obsessive, they are prepared, and they are objective about their results. You must have the discipline to celebrate only after you've accomplished what you say you will do. But here you are taking lots of cheat meals, cheat breaks, cheat days, and always underestimating discipline, principals, and consistency. Stop cheating, stop wasting time, and put your time and your money where your mouth is.

Stop celebrating when you are just average. Don't cheat after one hard day's work. If you had one long day at work and you're celebrating - that's just average. You need to have purposeful, consistent, and results-oriented long days at work over an extended period in order to celebrate. Hunker down now and celebrate after you've gotten the results that you want in life, sales, management, fitness, sports, or in your marriage and kids. Right now, you can't afford to cheat, you haven't built up the skill, discipline, and character yet, and you don't have the failures to solidify your belief in yourself yet. You are consistently partying, consistently cheating, consistently avoiding the grind and consistently looking for the easy path. What you need to do is consistently work hard towards your goals without cheating. Even if you are taking incre-Mental baby steps, the key is to make it consistent, then increase the intensity as you go. Show up every day consistently. You don't have to set personal records every day and every time you step onto the court of life, but you do need to be consistent. Small performances done consistently over time will yield greater results than high performance done inconsistently. Stop being a consistent cheater and partier, be a consistent Shower Upper.

You might want to ask yourself, "Will I be happy doing this same thing for the rest of my life? And am I going to do anything about it?" Sometimes asking what's important is what is required of you – no matter how scary it might be. Personally, I had to give up a really nice job so I can be uncomfortable for a while, lose everything, and almost die before I finally had the courage to own up to everything that has ever happened to me and find the balls to do what was required of me.

So, I ask you, what are you willing to sacrifice to follow your dreams and achieve them? Will you give up some sleep? Will you give up some fun? Will you give some comfort? Will you give up some negativity?

Will you give up some partying? Will you give up fishing? Will you give up your Smartphone and get off Facebook, Instagram, Snapchat, and Buzzfeed? Will you give up some time to concentrate on yourself and do what you what is required so you can live the life you want? Do you need to stop complaining? Do you need to ask for help? Do you need to give up some addictions and choose life? Do you need to read some books? Do you need to make time for yourself, to make a solid plan of action and follow through with it, with massive commitment and consistency?

If you are suffering, if you are getting nowhere in life, if you are in pain, if you are miserable, if you are not entirely happy, if you are not where you want to be, if things aren't working out as you planned, then you need to really take a look at yourself, be honest with yourself, and make the time to answer these questions. Do what's required.

Most of the time, you're not suffering enough to make the necessary change. Most of the time, you're just not in enough pain. Most of the time, you're just not miserable enough to change. Obviously, from your lack of purposeful action, you aren't scared enough. Evidently, you prefer mediocrity more than success. The truth is that if you choose what you have now over choosing to change it, then you can say what you want, but you just don't want success bad enough. If you did, you would do it already. Everything else is just excuses.

My cousin, Mang, told me in a conversation recently that he was scared of staying the same – tired, poor, dumb, afraid, living paycheck to paycheck – and I told him he obviously wasn't scared enough because he hasn't done anything different to change his results. He was shocked. Nobody ever told him the #truth. I told him there's nothing shocking about it. It's just insanity to think that you will do the same thing over and over and expect a different result each time. It's like a math equation. If you keep putting in the same numbers like 1+1, you'll always get 2. You're insane if you keep putting the same efforts of 1+1 and expecting your results to be 100. That's just asinine. Insanity. For your life to change, you need to put in some combination of effort that will equal 100, like 1+99 or 50+50, or any variable of effort that will get you the result you want. "But I'm trying!" Again, trying does not matter, you must do what is required to get the results you are looking for, that's it.

The pain of staying the same must be greater than the pain of change for you to succeed. You must want it bad enough. When you want it bad enough, you can finally be All In and do what is required of you, no matter how hard, how long, how much money it's going to take, no matter how far behind you are, and no matter what you know or don't know.

These days, ignorance is not an excuse, because there's a great thing called Google, or Barnes and Nobles, or The Library for those old schoolers – which has millions of books and information about every single subject you could ever hope to be an expert in. Google it, YouTube it, read about it, ask other people about it. For example, you want to be a fit or want a six-pack? Google it, there's millions of videos on workouts, diets, motivation, and meal plans – day by day, step by step. If you suck as sales as I once did, you Google it, YouTube it, read about it, ask other people about it. You will be overwhelmed with how much information is on the internet, open source and all! It has everything you need to be a great sales rep if you are All In and do what is required of you. It could just be as simple as searching for someone you want to be like and copying them. They will have tons of information, step by step of what it took, and how they did it. Then you read and watch everything they say and do, write it all down, plan it, and take SLGPPD action until you succeed. Copy their habits because you are your habits – not what you think you are or what you would like other people to think of you as.

That's what I did with Brian Tracy. He's the most polished and well put-together sales guy I've ever seen. He was the one guy I aspired to be when I started in the sales game. CEO-Type. Tall, good-looking, sharp, well spoken, off the charts smart! Everything I am not. But I admired him to no end as the prototypical sales guru that I wanted to be exactly like. Zig is pretty damn good too, I'd take Zig as well.

Now, obviously, you are not going to be that person immediately overnight. It might take years. Heck, it might take a whole lifetime, but if you want it bad enough, you will find a way. If not, you will surely find a reason to quit. Start now. Don't worry about all the details of how. There's no exact how anyway. The how is not the important thing and seldom yields the same results for you or others. You'll figure out the exact details later as you get better. Getting hung up in the details before starting is like planning exactly how to spend your lottery winnings without ever buying a lottery ticket. Just start now with a general plan and a powerful purpose. You want to be a successful chef? You want to be a business man? You want to be a stem cell researcher? You want to have a wonderful marriage? You want to be a bodybuilder? You want to be a great sales rep? You want to be a great manager? You want to be a great whatever? If you truly want it, you will Google it, you will YouTube it, you will ask people about it, you will not fear it, you will not care how long it takes, you will not care how much money it takes, you will do whatever it takes, you will do what is required of you to find the answers you are looking for. "I don't know" will not be an excuse anymore. You will just perform. All In.

You must perform. Your intentions do not matter. Your ideas do not matter. Everyone's got ideas, but ideas aren't worth a damn unless someone actually puts in the necessary work to make those ideas a reality. The ultimate proof is in the pudding. Did you make the time and the money for it? What have you actually produced? If my intentions did matter, my wife would understand. All those years of fighting and punching through walls, all those years of pain and suffering, all those years of being an ass and not knowing how to be a good husband, and all those years where I could have had so much more...sex.

My kids would understand if intentions mattered. They would have understood that Baba was busy. They would have stopped climbing all over my back. They would have stopped telling me to take them out to play. They would have cared if I was successful or not.

My bank account would understand. Just by having a great idea that nobody else has acted on, I would have been rich if not for the fact that I was scared and didn't do anything about it. Makes sense, right? Just by sheer want, sheer intention, I should have an immense bank account, right? It made sense to me at the time.

My intentions and ideas would actually impact people. I would be able to change lives out of intentions. Magically, out of my head, the world would change for the better! But that's not how life works. You say you want to do something, you say you will, you better because otherwise it just goes to your grave with you. Do what is required of you, there is no try.

Chapter 17 #Truths

- Your best is not enough, you must do what's required
- All you have in this world is your balls and your word, don't break them for no one!
- Give up the past, stop breaking your own balls
- Follow these two golden rules for any result you want in life:
  - #1) Just do what you say you're going to do
  - #2) Do what you don't want to do or what others won't do
- If it was easy, everyone would be successful
- Ask yourself true questions about what you really want in life and what you must do
- You can't afford to cheat when you're not great yet
- What are you willing to sacrifice?
- Small things done consistently will yield greater results than big things done inconsistently.
- Your input must be equal to your output
- These days with Google, "I don't know" is not an excuse
- Just perform, stop using intention as an excuse

Chapter 18: There is No Try

I just saw Kevin Durant, professional NBA basketball player of the Oklahoma Thunder, lose Game 7 of the 2016 Western Conference Basketball Finals, after being up 3-1 in the series against the Golden State Warriors. If trying mattered, I guarantee you that Kevin Durant would have at least two championship rings already. Maybe one day, he would stop trying and just do what is required of him. In this world, trying doesn't get you anywhere. Nobody sees you trying and nobody cares because everyone is trying. But very few do it. Doing is all that matters. That's why you don't get extra points for trying. That's why the top players and talents on this planet make so much money, because they perform and do what is required of them, even though other good players aren't that far behind in terms of stats. Michael Jordan went 6 for 6, that's what mattered, that's why he's the GOAT, the Greatest Of All Time. Except for Malone and Stockton, nobody cares about Malone or Stockton coming up short against Jordan. Performance is all that matters. Execution is all that matters. Keeping your word is all that matters.

Keeping your word and honoring your commitments are all that matters, not your intentions, not your ego, not what you say you WERE going to do, or all your trying. If you say you're going to do something, nobody will care unless you do it. Only you care if you try, but as we all know, if you really look at the #truth and own it, you'll realize that what we often think we are doing as enough, is not enough. Obviously, we always think we are doing better than we are and we are trying more than we really are. It's the only way some people are able to sleep at night or look at themselves in the mirror.

Like when I started working out, I never weighed myself much or counted my calories. I always just guesstimated that I was around the ball park. Later on, I realized was that when I actually cared enough to measure myself and my results accurately, I was actually 500 plus calories over every single day. I just conveniently forgot to count the gummy bears and Starbucks frappes. I would conveniently forget to do certain workouts that I know I'm weak in.

Same in golf, management, or sales…or just about anything else in life.

In golf, I have many a golfer friends who started playing around the same time or many years before me but could never break 100. They absolutely love golf. They try hard at it, too. They talk about it all the damn time and watch all major tournaments. They know all the rules and intricacies of golf. Some have even gotten some golf lessons and a golf coach or two. Some practice regularly, maybe a couple of times a week and play once a week. My buddy, Lu, buys new clubs every year – promising me that he's gotten an extra 15 yards on all his clubs and this year will be the year he beats me. My buddy Dee, has been changing his swing every year for God knows how long now. He once had a dependable slice game, then it turned into a nasty hook game, and now it's a reliable bullet grounder game. A boss of mine plays…well…boss golf. Boss golf is where you're the boss or the big customer and you are never out of bounds, never lost a ball, never count your bad shots, never have a bad lie, never have a bad game unless someone else is cheating, and anything from 6 feet in is a gimme…because you can and no one is going to say otherwise. All these folks have three things in common: they suck, they don't keep score, and they try. When you boil it all down, they suck because they just try but not hard enough – they don't do what's required. They don't own the #truth that they are not as good as they think they are so they never do what's required to get the results they say they want.

In sales, when I used to suck, I would always think I was doing good and trying real hard, but when the numbers came out every month, I'd be surprised that I was way behind budget. The worst when I found myself in a hole already early in the year. I'd reason that it was still early and I'd have the months of summer and fall to catch up. When I finally stopped trying, owned the #truth, started measuring my actual results, I realized that pointless activities for the sake of trying, feeling, and looking like you're doing something productive is a waste of time. It's a waste of time because it gets no real results that matter, in any part of my life.

My wife would have understood when I tried to be a good husband, but was always late. My kids would have understood when I tried to be a good father, but never showed up to play with them. My boss would have understood that I tried to hit my sales budget but came up short again. Everyone would understand that I tried to be a good sales rep, but always ends up clapping and never walked the stage. Oh, but I tried. I would have been the CEO of my previous employer now if they counted me trying, bleeding, and stressing. I would be rich beyond my wildest dreams if trying was the measurement.

Here's the thing, everyone tries, but few do. One of the greatest philosophers in history, Master Yoda from Star Wars fame, said, "Do or do not, there is no try." In this world, there are only two types of people: Those who do and those who try. Trying is the most overused excuse in the history of mankind. Doing your best is the world in which most people live in. It's romantic. It's cute. It's just people lying to themselves so they can go to sleep at night. The world meets nobody halfway. If you want something, you have to go out there and get it because I promise you it is not going to come to you. If you really want it, it doesn't matter how far, how hard, how expensive, and how long, you will find a way. If you don't, you will always find a reason to quit and you'll always just try. If you really want something you'll make time and money for it. You'll perform rather than make excuses if it's really something you care about. You'll explore all options even if it's uncomfortable. Call it what you want - addiction, obesity, procrastination, laziness, ignorance, or mediocrity – unless you believe, you own up to it, and do what is required of you, it will be nothing more than just an excuse. Stop trying. There is no try.

Chapter 18 #Truths

- Execution and keeping your word is key.
- People always think they're doing better than they really are unless they measure themselves objectively
- Do or do not; there is no try
- Stop trying, just do it

Chapter 19: I Love My Kids

Many people say they love their kids and their parents but their actions prove otherwise. They do everything the same as they've always done. They're scared, but not scared enough. They are living month to month, no savings whatsoever, working their asses off for the man, year after year, decade after decade, and usually a whole life time. When asked what they want, they usually say it's to be able to provide for their kids and their family above all else. They say they will do whatever it takes because their love is unconditional. Unfortunately, doing what they have always done has only gotten them to this point. Some people really believe that doing the same thing over and over will get them the results they are looking for even if the past 10 years has proved otherwise. I ask them what their plans are to provide for their kids, they can't tell me. Some will tell me they will just work harder. I ask them, "Really? How? And how has that been working for you?" They can't tell me. So, I ask them, "So you're just going to work harder at doing what you've always done to get you where you don't know where you want to go?" Usually just silence.

The #truth is that if you don't do what is required of you, you will never get to where you want to go – if you even know where you want to go or how to get there. Most people say they love their kids. They say they will do anything for their kids, except for doing whatever it truly takes to make it happen and become the person they want to be. They instead just go hunting, fishing, shopping, gambling, drinking, partying, or hobbying almost every day during the seasons. They spend all their money and savings on their hobbies, indulgences, addictions, and distractions. They preach about their kids needing to do what they say and not what they do.

They have new cars when they should have new jobs. They have new toys when they should have new purpose.

I believe a parent who could, should love their kids by being All In on striving to ensure that their kids never have to be burdened by lack of money, love, or approval to be happy. I most certainly understand that sometimes it is incredibly tough for parents to take care of their children the way they would like to with their current situations in life. They somehow someway just got behind, were given very little opportunity, the timing was just off, were dealt some bad hands, and are just not where they want to be yet. Most believe it to be their supreme duty to make sure their kids are going to be fine financially and morally when they leave this life so they keep working so hard. This was the case with my parents. Because they love me so much, now that I have kids of my own, I'm determined to make sure my parents don't have to work so hard anymore. As of right now, it seems I don't love them enough and I am not doing enough because my parents are still working so hard from 3 A.M. to 10 P.M. every day from Spring to Fall and they are already close to retirement age. I need to be All In on making sure my family is taken cared of so that we can maximize the time we have been miraculously given to spend with each other before it's gone. That is why I must work harder now because I'm not there yet, and the sooner I succeed, the more time I will have to spend with my loved ones.

Here's one of my most feared scenarios: You have kids that are 10 and 8 years old, you are dead broke, living from paycheck to paycheck, you've got massive credit card debt, your parents are dead broke so you have to take care of them, your siblings are dead broke, you can barely make it to work and back because you're always tired, you don't read, you don't write, you don't learn, you don't invest, you only work so that you can relax and sleep in all day on the weekends, have a little fun, then you do it all over again. How has the past 10 years of doing the same thing been working for you? What makes you think that in 8 to 10 years when your kids want to go to college, that you can afford it? How would you feel having to tell your kids that you didn't do what you should have done years ago to support them? Don't worry about how they will feel. Worry about how sorry you will feel. That's when you will know if you really loved them or not, and you'll have an even more incredibly tough road ahead. I wouldn't know how to live after facing that disappointment from my kids. All you needed to do was stop the BS excuses and do what is required of you to provide for them, but you didn't, you'd rather live in pity, ignorance, comfort, past, fear, and blame. By then, you will regret the things you didn't do and that pain will be greater than the pain you have now. The good news is there's always time, Bolo. It's never too late if you're not mathematically over yet.

There are certain rhythms to life depending on where you live, but certainly in most developed countries there's this rhythm that is almost assured to make you successful. There's so many ways to succeed and there's always exceptions, but from what I've seen in all my years of observing successful people, most successful people follow a certain pattern in life here in America. You spend the first half of your life building and acquiring, then spend the second half of your life giving it away. In your 20's, you learn as much as you can, from small companies and big companies. You learn how to learn. You learn about who you are. You seek mentors. You make a lot of mistakes. You take a lot of risks. You work your ass off, get really good at something, and build momentum into your thirties. In your 30's, you work your ass off even harder. You become an expert at something. You create something and build something. You don't ask for an easier job that pays a little more, don't ask for less responsibilities, instead you work hard on a legacy so you'll be ready to collect in your forties. In your 40's, you maximize these prime money-making years. You focus on the things that you've built. You maximize that nest you've been building for decades, and try not to make any big mistakes that's going to set you back to such an extent that you can't recover. In your 50's, you need to just focus on protecting your nest, your equity, and your legacy. Now is the maximum time to give back, teach, and mentor. In your 60's and beyond, you should already be retired, be spending as much time with your grandkids as possible, explore, travel, relax, spend money on yourself, check off the last items off the bucket list, enjoy the fruits of your labor, and give back to the world that has given to you before you die.

If you are in front, keep doing what you're doing and don't let up, keep your eyes on the prize. If you're ten or fifteen years behind, why the hell are you still so tired, why are you still trying to sleep in peacefully every day, why are you still drinking or smoking, why are you not angry, why are you taking naps, why are you on social media, why are you watching TV, why are you relaxing or hanging out on the weekends, what are you celebrating exactly, why are you taking it easy, why aren't you scared, why are you still lolly-gagging at the start when everyone else is lapping you? You should be running as fast as you can, harder than anyone else in front of you. You should be hungry as hell. You should be working your ass off day and night to catch up if you are behind like my parents were 18 years ago and as I am now. You should be making plans and doing what is required of you.

You can say you love your kids all you want with your words, but without action, you don't really love your kids. Everyone says they love their kids and they will do whatever it takes to provide for them, but many don't do it. Action is all that matters, intentions are not enough. I don't know is an excuse. Trying is an excuse. Doing your best for your kids is just an excuse. Like the old saying goes, Excuses are like assholes, everyone's got one. You don't love your kids, you just love saying you love your kids. If you were poor like I was, you live in America or any developed country, and you have kids who you love, you will do whatever it takes to be successful and make sure they never have to suffer like you did. That's real love. If you have poor habits, if you have poor actions, if you have a poor mindset, and you love your kids, why the hell are you not running as fast as you can? Why aren't you out there knocking on doors, making friends, taking names, landing jobs, and doing whatever it takes and being All In.

For my parents, I was 18 years old and about to head off to college when they took a real hard look at their savings, their work, their legacy, and decided that they were already so far behind and they weren't going to have enough finances to help my brother and I through college or out of college when we go on our own. I was already on my way to college and my brother would be as well after two more years. Yeah, they could have said, "Oh well, we're Hmong, we're poor, we've suffered so much tragedy, we came to America in our early thirties while having to take care of our parents and kids, we're just so behind in everything, it's perfectly logical, reasonable, understandable, and excusable if we don't succeed." But they didn't. They owned up to exactly what their situation was. They didn't dramatize it. They took responsibility. They did what was required of them to succeed, and they persevered until they succeeded. No excuses.

My mom was 39 and my dad was 42 years old already by the time I graduated high school. They had spent their first 10 years in America learning the language, the culture, and the customs, and building their skills and knowledge. They weren't nearly as ready as most people born here, but they had no choice so they took a chance and bought a farm, and tried learning how to build a tough business literally from the ground up. Their only reference was driving down to Fresno, California and talking to a Hmong strawberry stand farmer about how to grow strawberries. Then the next day they started looking for land and found a 10-acre piece, by the grace of God, by driving around and asking everyone and anyone. Lo and behold! They took what little savings they had, invested everything in it, and became farmers. All In. It happened rather quickly. Never underestimate what you can do in one day. Everyone thought they were crazy, even my brother and me. I will never question them again after that. But they still had to keep their day jobs to make ends meet. And they worked, oh my goodness, did they ever work. I've never seen or heard of two human beings working so hard in my entire life and I'm not sure I ever will. They did what was required of them so that they could have extra income to help their kids. The first five years are always the toughest in anything people do, especially in business. That's the time that counts the most. The blood, sweat, tears, learning curve, tough choices and decisions, hunger, stress, fear, sacrifice, wanting to quit, and persistence and perseverance were an everyday occurrence – usually all of it together. It took them a whole decade to be able to survive purely off their business and could both quit their day jobs. My brother and I would have understood if they didn't work as hard, but they wouldn't. They would not have been able to forgive themselves had they not done everything humanly possible to stop the buck of poverty from going any further than them. Now that's real true love – doing superhuman things because it was required of them. They didn't have time to be sorry and scared. They only had time to do whatever it takes. When you're All In, that's what you do. Anything else would be distractions, excuses, and lies. They truly love their kids.

When my son was born in 2010, I finally understood real love. After 36 hours of labor, a bloody mess everywhere, my wife having to be sewn back up, and finally holding my little beautiful baby boy in my arms; suddenly, nothing else mattered. Not the condo that was under water and all the guilt. Not the looming credit card debt and all the unnecessary struggles. Not the corporate ladder that I was trying to climb and all the misery. Not the horrible sales results and the BS that I was telling myself about how pathetic I was. All that mattered was that I was going to do whatever it takes to care of this boy and his mom. I didn't know I could love her more than I already did, but seeing her endure such labor and pain, I love her more than ever and will continue loving her more and more each day and each time that I look at my son.

My mom was right all along. She always said, "Son, you don't know what real love means until you have children of your own." That woman is always right...again. So, I started my journey. It wasn't fast. It was most certainly not smooth. There was a lot of back and forth, a lot of mistakes, a lot of anger, a lot of pity, a lot of blame, a lot of revenge seeking, a lot of fear, a lot of doubt, a lot of tears, and a lot of sleepless nights.

Finally, after I decided I was going to be a man my son would be proud of, I took a trip by myself to Ojai, California. It was one of the best decisions I ever made. The first thing I did was draw. I hadn't touched a pencil in 15 years, even though I used to be pretty good before that. I made the time to be with myself so I can learn about myself and what's truly important to me. This specific action of taking time for me and isolating myself from all the noise was what was required of me at that moment. I started to learn the truth about myself. I started to stop the blaming. I started to own up and take responsibilities for everything that did or did not happen to me. I started to believe. I started to do what was required of me where I was at in life. I had to start sacrificing. I got back to basics. I looked back at my life and really analyzed what made me successful and what didn't. I thought about what was important to me – truly important, none of the nonsense and the noise. I wrote down what I wanted in life. It was the first time I wrote something down that wasn't on a Post-it note and didn't lose it. I made a plan, a real plan of action: one that started with the end in mind, one that spanned my whole life, one that was detailed, and one that had specific and measurable actions, deadlines, results, and milestones.

It would take me 5 years from deciding, suffering, learning, planning, taking a giant leap of faith, taking massive action, failing, losing everything, being scared, almost committing suicide, learning again, and being grateful to get where I'm at right now. I'm more successful than I've ever imagined, but not as successful as I believe I can be.

For most people, doing what is required could be just as simple as taking one hour to sit back – with no cellphones, no friends, no family, no TV, nothing – to make some time for yourself, to be with yourself, to think about and write down what is really important to you, and then do that thing and don't quit until you succeed. Unfortunately, most of us can't do that or won't do that. We are so busy and caught up in the everyday transactions of this society that we can't allocate time for ourselves. Most people don't like to be alone with their own thoughts. They have to always be doing something – playing on their phones (even while eating out with family and friends), watching TV, listening to the radio, anything other than being with themselves and truly hearing what's going on inside. I'm not talking about what you heard, what your friends said, what your affiliations told you, what the media makes it out to be, what the internet tells you…I'm talking about a real investigative search into your own soul, your own past, your own experiences, and researching what is real, what is made up, what is interpreted, and what you decide to care about and commit to. That generally shows up in where you spend your time and your money and just about everything else in your life. That's what I look at when a person says they care about something or what they intend to do or what they are already doing. That's where I generally find out the real #truth. And then after all of that, believing, owning up, after all the sacrificing and doing what is required of you…then comes the hard part, the NEVER GIVING UP.

Chapter 19 #Truths

- If you truly love your kids or your parents, you should be all in on being successful and your actions will align with your words
- Be aware of the rhythms of success
- If you're behind, you should be running faster to catch up
- Be all in on finding out what's important to you then do whatever it takes to make sure you achieve it
- For most people to succeed, they just have to stop all the distractions and focus

Step 4: Never Give Up

"You just can't beat the person who never gives up"

-Babe Ruth

Chapter 20: Everyone Has What It Takes

All of you have what it takes to succeed. Don't ever give up, because if I can do it, I know you can do it. In high school, I succeeded because I believed and most importantly, I did not give up, no matter how tough it got. I wasn't that special, I wasn't a school genius like my brother. I was not an athletic freak. I was not great at anything in particular.

The only reason I was succeeded was because I did what was required of me and I did not give up when it got tough. I didn't let my bad English stop me. I didn't make excuses. I owned up to what I was up against, kept getting better, and never gave up. I knew that I was disadvantaged. I was learning my ABC's in the third grade when everyone was reading big books already. But one day at a time, consistently, I got better and better, and I believed that I was going to be valedictorian. Trust me, I am not that special, but when I know what I really want, I will do whatever it takes to get it, and you're going to have to kill me to stop me because I will outlast you. It has always been a blessing and a curse. My wife reminds me of it all the time – she calls it Stupid Stubborn though.

Just like how I used to play tennis. I beat most of the number one players from other schools even though I was so far behind because I never learned how to do anything properly. I never even learned how to serve the ball and serving is pretty important in tennis. My coach used to say, "Kao, for everyone else, their serve is an asset, for you, it's a liability!" The plan was to tap it back to the opponents' backhands, then run back to the middle, and rely on my speed and tenacity to chase down the balls so I could tap it back to their backhands time and time again. After about 4 or 5 live balls, they would get frustrated and hit it out or into the net. I only had one strategy…to wear them the hell out! They may be taller, stronger, and played at a country club since they were a kid, but they're not going to outwork me. Even if they don't know, I knew. I believed in my heart of hearts that they've never had to work as hard as me and they've never suffered like I did, so they're not going to beat me unless they are just several levels better. It helps that they've never played against anyone as determined as me before and they underestimated me every single time. That was my secret to success early on – massive determination and people always underestimating me. Being small, quick, flexible, determined, with nothing to lose, and grossly underestimated can be a big advantage. I was able to turn that into being the number tennis player on my team, All-league, and All-Sections.

I always compared myself to David from the David and Goliath Bible story. David was small, quick, flexible, determined, with nothing to lose, and grossly underestimated. Goliath was big and strong but his victories had caused him to be slow and lazy so he overestimated David. Goliath's greatest strength was his greatest weakness. His own victories defeated him. Goliath is the big guy, the rich guy, the privileged guy, the good-looking guy, the polished and perfect sales rep guy, and the guy who had won all his life because of how he was born. David is me, the small guy, the poor, the disadvantaged, the ridiculed, the loser, the guy who had to claw for everything he got (every freakin' little sale), the guy who had to work ten times harder for the same results as those other guys, and most likely, some of you folks who are reading this book. If you're like me, you usually don't have anything to lose, nothing really holding you down - you are fast, agile, able to move quickly, people always underestimating you, you can just step back and swing as many times as it takes, and eventually you'll knock something out.

Eventually, on a long enough timeline, if you do what's required, if you don't quit, if you persevere, if you go All In, you will succeed. It's just a matter of time. Everyone has what it takes to be successful.

Chapter 20 #Truths

- You have everything it takes to succeed
- Being an underdog is not exactly a bad thing
- One simple strategy, done consistently and with massive determination, will yield very good results
- Even if you're not there yet, on a long enough timeline, if you do what's required and don't quit, you are guaranteed success

Chapter 21: Determination

"Nothing in this world can take the place of persistence. Talent will not: nothing is more common than unsuccessful men with talent. Genius will not; unrewarded genius is almost a proverb. Education will not: the world is full of educated derelicts. Persistence and determination alone are omnipotent." –Calvin Coolidge

Ladies and gentlemen, determination is the number one factor between successful people and unsuccessful people - not money, not skills, not knowledge, not resources, not knowing people. It's really simple, given a long enough timeline you will succeed if you keep playing. You only fail permanently if you quit. Most people quit every time it gets tough. Success is usually right over the next mountain, my people used to say, but most never find it because they turned back already. Just like in fitness, I've known friends who go to the gym for a year but stay exactly the same size as when they first started. That's because they quit every time it gets hard or when hit their first plateau. They never do one more rep on any set. In fact, they quit way before that, they quit when they remotely start to strain. They'll make excuses like, I'm just doing circuit workouts, Bro. They never get sore. Without getting sore, you will never grow. The same goes for sales and life. Sometimes you have to be sore for a really really long time to succeed. But trust me, it's not going to kill you. In fact, it's a good thing, and many times, it means you know you're doing the right thing.

Because I had been through so much, I love telling all my new hire reps when they come to me and express how much they're struggling, Good, welcome to Sales, that means you're doing something right, now go and struggle some more. I tell them how I've struggled and wanted to quit so many times and looking back, every time I didn't quit, it was always the right decision. I struggled my way out of it. Because I struggled so much and didn't give up, I eventually became better than I ever thought possible.

Take my parents for instance. After coming to America with zero red cents in their pockets, zero language, zero education, zero work experience, zero knowledge of the culture and customs, zero driving skills, and zero help and support from anyone…they managed to provide for our family. They had to take care of two naughty boys and my grandparents - support all four of us and themselves in a brand-new country! They took every single kind of job imaginable to make ends meet - from church volunteer, to seamstress, walnut picker, farm worker, to carpenter, to dishwasher, to fiberglass pusher, to fire-stomper, to janitor, to grass-mower, to librarian volunteer, to librarian assistant, to teacher's aide and bus driver, getting passed over and over by people who they trained.

Then after toiling aimlessly for 10 years in America, they saw a great deal on some land so they decided to become farmers, hoping that it would lead to something better. They had no clue how to farm in America! Everyone thought they were crazy – me, my brother, my Grandpa, all my uncles and aunts, and everyone I knew. I heard my grandparents and uncles talk so much crap about my parents that I even remembered being embarrassed for them. But they didn't listen to anyone. It was such hard work, especially the first couple of years because they had absolutely no equipment. All the strawberry trenches had to be dug by hand! I know, because I helped dig many of those damn trenches.

They sacrificed for years before making any money. They just kept believing and kept on being determined. They worked their asses off to a degree I've never seen anyone else ever do. The first five years were the absolute toughest! They still had their day jobs. They would wake up at 2 A.M., prepare, go to the farm at 3 A.M., work in the dark with their helmet lights on until about 8 A.M., then go to their day jobs. At around noon, they would go open the stand, work for 45 minutes or so, then go back to their day jobs until 4 or 5 P.M., then go back to the farm and work their butts off until 9 or 10 P.M. every weekday, except in the winter time where they might get some reprieve. On Saturdays and Sundays, they would work even harder because it was busier. Seven days a week, no weekends off, no vacations…all for my brother and I. Words can never, ever, absolutely, positively be enough to ever thank them and repay them for all they've done for my me and brother. If anyone asks them why they work so hard, even the city newspaper, my parents would say it was a vacation every single day on the farm. They just kept believing and being determined. They were All In on the American Dream.

It took about five years before they really started figuring out exactly what type of plants and vegetables thrived and how to make money. My dad was able to quit his day job and they finally started to realize their dream.

After ten years, they were finally successful and my mom was able to quit her day job. However, she paid for it with skin cancer of the face. It was a stressful time, and she had to have surgery to cut away the affected areas of her face and graft it together from other areas of her body. She was heavily medicated and told to stay home for a month, but she was out there the very next day under a huge hat – delirious, in pain, and sweating through the Vaseline covering her face. It was brutal. I didn't understand why or how much she suffered back then.

My mom toiling in the 105-degree dry heat with her makeshift face protector

My handsome father taking a much-deserved break by his shack at the farm

My father's dream come true

Now that I have two boys of my own, I finally understand now why my parents work so hard even if they don't really have to anymore. I know now why they never quit even when they understandably should have. I know now why they always have hope even when it was bleak. I know now why they always tell my brother and I they love us every single day even when we got tired of hearing it. I know now why they are such good people when very few were good to them. I know now why they have no bad habits except for over-working. I know now why they don't fear people and people's opinions of them. I know now why they are so strong. I know now why they don't like to waste time and opportunity. And I finally know now why they wanted my brother and I to be proud of them…to be such great parents, examples, role models, and heroes. They showed me that I can do more than just survive in this world, that I can be an example of the fearlessness and strength it takes to change the world for the better. My only goal in life now is to show my kids the same thing. Perhaps I will not change the world, end world hunger, or achieve world peace, but I will be such an example of guts and fearlessness that my kids will have the opportunity to so.

Enter my uncle and aunt in Visalia, California. They didn't even know anything about the restaurant business when they started. They called the restaurant, simply, Pho N Seafood. Straight to the point. They believed in their dream of owning a restaurant so much that they leveraged their house, their parent's house, their brothers' houses, and borrowed a lot of money from anyone and everyone. They didn't make any money for 3 years. They all still had to keep their day jobs, they all had to take shifts from their day jobs, and they sacrificed all the sleep and free time they could afford just to make ends meet. All the kids had to help as low-paid or mostly free servers and dishwashers. There was a point at which everything seemed lost and they were about to start all over again. My aunt would still tell me to this that if they gave up many times and if they knew better, if they knew how hard it was going to be, they would never have started. However, if they gave up entirely, they would have lost all their houses, all their life savings, and would have been homeless. Only through five years of sheer determination, hard work, persistence, and perseverance that they succeeded.

The best Asian soul food restaurant in the world (Pho N Seafood, Visalia, CA)

The late and great, Jerry Maras, was one of my best friends, brother, customer, mentor, and teacher. He taught me about how to love your wife and kids. He taught me so much about paint, business, sales, marriage, life, and how to play golf, but not just that, he taught me about focus. Always about focus. Focus, Cali! Don't focus on the shit, Cali! Always focus on your own game, Cali! Don't worry about what I'm doing, Cali! Focus on what you need to do right now, Cali! Focus only on this one shot, Cali! Focus! Focus! Focus! It was always about focus, on the golf course and in life, and always about what's truly important – which was taking care of your family and friends and keeping your word. Even though he was divorced, he would always say that his ex-wife was, is, and always will be The One. She was, His Girl. Nothing would ever change that. Even though things didn't work the way he had pictured, he gave her his word, he promised her for better or for worse, so he would take care of her until the day he died. And he did. He never needed much, except to take care of his family and friends and brothers, and to play golf. He told me I had everything it takes to be a great golfer and to be great at anything in life – the fearlessness and the willingness to learn, to practice, to get better, but more importantly, to never give up.

Jerry Freaking Maras counting how many holes and how much money he won, as usual

The greatest game of my life was with Jerry. He was a scratch golfer and I was a 17 handicap so he had to give me 17 shots – basically a shot a hole on the 17 toughest holes during this match-play tournament game. The first eight holes at our club, Shorecliffs Golf Course in San Clemente – his second home, were especially brutal for me that day. I had nothing, absolutely nothing. I was shanking and hooking left and right. My chipping was atrocious and I couldn't putt to save my life. Not a single par was made or in sight during those first eight holes. Jerry was his usual self – pars and birdies – always applying the pressure, never giving me a break, but always encouraging me at the same time, and always being the consummate player. He wasn't a golfer, he was a player. He'd always say that he didn't have the natural striking ability of a pure golfer, but he was born to play. Everyone always said, Jerry Freaking Maras, that guy is a player! And what a player he was!

I didn't win or tie a single hole at all for eight holes. He was up 8 holes and we only had 10 more holes left to play. We came to one of the toughest hole on the course, the dog-leg right par-4 9th hole and my head was a mess. My confidence was shot. I was all but done.

I heard him say as he always does when I'm getting my ass kicked, "Cali, round ball round hole, anything can happen! Put the wall up! As long as you're not mathematically over, you still got a shot! One hole at a time! One shot at a time, Cali! Come on, you can do it, grind it out! Keep grinding, Cali!"

So, I took a deep breath, slowed down my heart, reached deep down, and focused only on my next shot. I finally hit a long, straight drive, but I hit it too far and it ran all the way to the edge of the creek at the end of the fairway. I couldn't hit my next shot normal right handed because it was unplayable with thick shrubbery, water, and overhanging trees. That meant I had to turn my six-iron over and hit the ball left-handed that was sitting under some tree branches, right by the edge of the creek. I flushed it down the middle to near the front of the green. All day I couldn't hit an iron normally, but left-handed I was able to flush it. Go figure. I topped my chip a bit but luckily it stopped five feet past the hole and I sank the putt for par. Jerry made par too, but he was giving me a shot so I won the hole. Jerry just laughed at the improbability of it all. Of all the holes, I chose to beat him on that hole by the most unusual means possible. I had nothing all day, then I almost put it in the creek, then had to hit left-handed, then chipped on while not being able to chip the whole front nine, and then made a putt which I couldn't even smell for eight holes, against a player as great as he was. Impossible in most cases; especially against someone like Jerry and especially the horrible way I was playing all day.

Renewed, I went on to par the 10th hole and won over Jerry's par. Then I birdied the par-5 11th out of nowhere with a putt off the green and won over Jerry's kick-in birdie.

Mad with confidence, I pushed my next drive into the crap up on the hill to the right on the par-5 12th hole and had to re-tee with a weak shot to the left near the hazard. From there, I proceeded to chunk one down to the middle about 150 yards away from the hole, laying four. Then I hit my fifth shot short of the front and had to putt my sixth shot off the green, uphill past the hole, with a fast and tough 4-footer coming back down, but luckily, I made it for seven. Jerry was long and down the middle as usual off the tee. But the most unusual thing happened, he hit one down the right side that ran into the Out-of-Bounds and had to go back and re-drop where he originally hit it from. Then he hits it close to the same spot; fortunately, it didn't go out of bounds, but he had to chip off some dirt and leaves which left his shot short of the green. Laying five, he two-putted off the green, and made seven to lose to my seven. All day he didn't sniff anything near a bogie. At this point, he was up 5 with six holes to play.

On the tough, long, uphill par-3 13th hole, I put my tee shot into the front left bunker and he puts his on the green as usual and two-putted for par. I got out of the bunker past the hole and two-putted for bogie to push with Jerry. However, now Jerry is up 5 with only five more holes to play. He's dormy, meaning I had to win every single hole to win – no ties or losses. There's no way for him to lose unless we go to play-offs. That's what I would have to do to beat him. Against anyone, it would be incredibly tough; against a player like Jerry, it was impossible. But I all I heard were his words, Focus, Cali!

On the short par-4 14th, we were both on the green in two, but his putt was in the middle and relatively short and easy for him, while I was far away, almost off the green on the right. Jerry barely missed the birdie putt and ended up with an easy tap-in par. I flubbed my putt short and had a difficult, down-hill sliding right to left 15-footer. I was a goner. Focus, Cali. Once again, one shot, do or die, on the brink of elimination, I was able to tap into something deep within when absolutely needed, with Jerry happily reminding me of the dire straits I was in, and buried the putt with authority and won the hole. Four down, four to play.

On the long par-3 15th hole, the pin was on the back shelf near a slope. Jerry hits it comfortably pin-high around 8 feet left of the pin and I hit it a little long and right off the green a few feet, and was left with a fast and tough 10-foot putt coming down. I hit it too hard, the ball ran past the hole, took the slope, and almost rolled off the green. Now I had an extremely hard uphill, breaking left 25-footer while Jerry had just missed his relatively easy birdie putt and kicked-in for par. Focus, Cali. Somehow the golf gods were with me again and I smashed it in to par it and beat him again. Everyone laughed while I screamed with excitement and relief. Three down, three to play.

On to the par-5 16th hole, I sliced my drive up the hill almost near the green of the last hole. I was in some rough and tall grass; amazingly though, the ball was sitting up! Unfortunately, the only shot I had was to smash a clean three-wood, off a slightly downhill lie, keep the ball under some branches of a small tree in front of me to the right, over some tall bushes directly in front of that, through some tall trees behind that, and land it safely in the middle of the fairway because there was hazard beyond that. Of all the craziest shots I've ever attempted and made, that was above all, the most spectacular shot I've ever made or will probably ever make. The screaming I made after must have shook all of San Clemente like an earthquake. Jerry hit an almost equally impressive 9-iron shot clean and pure off the concrete hazard which was a V-shaped ditch running along the left side because he had pulled his drive a little bit and it took a bad bounce left into the ditch. Most people wouldn't even dream of such a shot, because they would have to stand with one foot in the ditch and one foot out, lift the club almost directly vertical, come down with such precision and accuracy to pick the ball clean, while trying not to break your club. There was barely a "tink" noise made because he picked it off so cleanly. I threw my hands up and yelled, "Oh my freakin' God, Jere'!" in disbelief. He landed near me in the middle of the fairway with about 125 yards to go. We both hit pitching wedge in. He lands in the middle, I chunk and end up short, while the flag was in the back. He rims out his birdie putt, kicks in his par, and proceeds to remind me that I haven't really hit a good chip all day. Focus, Cali. I take a deep breath and flush the most crucial and important chip of my life to within six inches, almost holing it, and winning the hole with a par. Two down, two to play.

The par-4 17th hole was the only hole where I don't have a stroke. It's one of the easiest holes on the course – straight and wide and short, slightly tucked into the left, guarded by a front right bunker. Jerry crushes one down the middle, and I crush one down the left side. The pin is right smack in the middle, but Jerry uncharacteristically hits his second shot short below the hole, barely on the green; however, it's an easy two-putt for him for par. I have to birdie to have any chance – meaning I have to hit a perfect 8-iron even though I haven't hit a clean iron shot all day and hadn't really hit a green in regulation the whole game. I flushed it to 3 feet and sank the putt with a grin, and its Jerry's turn to throw his hands ups.

We come to the par-4 18th, Jerry is only 1 up with one last hole to play. He tells me he's proud of me for grinding and fighting, but he's going to finish me off now. I gladly accept the challenge, saying back to him his famous words, "Round ball round hole, Jere, anything can happen! I'm gonna win this hole, then I'm gonna kick your ass in the play-off!"

We both hit it long and straight down the middle, I actually beat him by 10 yards and was ecstatic and I let him know that while he smiled. He hits it nicely to within 10 feet of the stick in the middle the green. I hit it pin-high but a few feet off the green to the left. I expected him to make birdie so I try to hole it off the green and run past the hole about five feet. He miraculously misses another relatively easy putt for him and settled for a par. I sank the hardest 5-footer of my entire life to win the hole.

We go to play-off on the first hole, a tough dog-leg left par 5.

We both drive it down the middle, he hits a beautiful second shot to about 120 yards while I hit a safe second shot and have about 150 yards left. He gets on the green as did I but fortunately he misses another relatively easy 12-foot birdie putt from the middle for par while I two-putt from 20 feet to win the hole with a net birdie and the match. It was the greatest game of my life and will probably be the greatest game ever in the history of mankind.

If you would have told me that I would have nothing on the front nine and had to get it together to come back to win against such improbably odds, I would have told you that they were freaking crazy. If you would have told me that I would have nothing on the front nine, had to come back against such improbably odds, and had to do it against Jerry Freaking Maras? I would slap you upside the head and put you down where you stand, that's just blasphemy, complete and utter nonsense, how dare you, impossible! That day was the greatest day of my life aside from the birth of my first son.

Because of that game and all Jerry taught me, when I was going through the toughest point of my life last year, I remembered what he would always say, "You're not mathematically over yet, Cali! Round ball, round hole, Cali, anything can happen!" and I put the wall up, grinded it out, focused on what's important, didn't quit, and finally got back up. When I got my life back together, he was the first person I called, and reflecting now, I'm just so happy I got the chance to tell him I loved him, and I thanked him.

Words will never be able to express how truly blessed I was to have had the chance in this life to know him and call him my Dear Friend and Brother. I will forever be grateful. He truly was a miracle to me and so many others. We would often joke that when we go, it'd be on the golf course - getting hit by a golf ball, rolling down a hill on a golf cart, struck by lightning, or our hearts would give out, but not our will, and if we could, we'd play in wheelchairs. I was glad he was with Gary, Kenny, and the boys when he did go, when his heart gave out over his will...on the golf course. He went the only way he knew how...birdie, birdie, eagle.

Jerry. Freaking. Maras.

Ask anyone who has ever succeeded and is successful in life or sales or business or family or anything, what the number one reason for their success is, and they will tell you it is DETERMINATION above all else. They will all tell you that they wanted to quit so bad, so many times, but they persevered and because of that sole reason...they succeeded.

Ladies and gentlemen, it's all about determination. It is not luck or something magical that they have and you don't. It's not a secret they are not telling you. It's just sheer, unsexy, unglamorous determination. That's why I succeeded and that is why you will succeed. By using these 4 simple steps, you will succeed in beating the odds in sales and in life: Step 1, Believe in Yourself; Step 2, Own It; Step 3, Do What is Required; and Step 4, Never Give Up.

Now you have all the tools you will ever need to become a great sales person, to become whatever you want to be and do whatever you want to do in life. Just don't waste it. Time does not wait for us, so do not wait for time. Do not waste this opportunity you have here in America, the greatest country in the world! Others have died, is dying, and will die for the opportunity that you have right in front of you. You can do whatever it is you want and nobody is going to stop you. Life is what you make of it so follow your dreams, be All In, and beat whatever odds that come your way.

Whatever you do, don't you ever give up because if you're reading this, you're not mathematically over yet...round ball, round hole, anything can happen.

Chapter 21 #Truths

- Nothing in this world can take the place of persistence
- You just can't beat the person who never gives up
- Determination is the number one factor between successful people and unsuccessful people
- Even if you start over with NOTHING 4 times, start again and believe like my parents
- It takes around 5 years for most successes to happen so don't quit
- Don't waste this opportunity you have that others would die for
- You're not mathematically over yet, round ball, round hole, anything can happen!
- Do it for Keng Yang, make him live forever

REFERENCES:

- Leung, Ho Hon, Lau, Raymond, Shaw-McEwen, Sharon with Rawlins, Susan M. *Investigating Diversity: Race, Ethnicity, and Beyond.* Cambridge, UK. Linton Atlantic Books, Ltd., 2008.
- August, 2016. Online, Internet, http://www.asian-nation.org/hmong.shtml.
- Lee, Cha Vue – Personal Interviews/Conversations. Long Beach, CA, Spring, 2015. Willows, CA, Summer, Fall, Winter, 2015, Spring, Summer, 2016.
- Yang, Cha Mee – Personal Interviews/Conversations. Long Beach, CA, Spring, 2015. Willows, CA, Summer, Fall, Winter, 2015, Spring, Summer, 2016.

Made in the USA
San Bernardino, CA
20 February 2018